A STRONGER KINSHIP

C. 1

A STRONGER KINSHIP

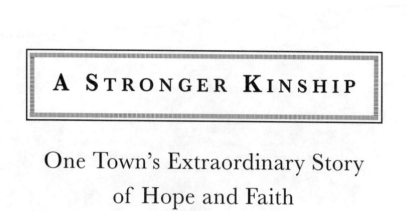

One Town's Extraordinary Story of Hope and Faith

Anna-Lisa Cox

Little, Brown and Company

NEW YORK   BOSTON

Little, Brown and Company
Time Warner Book Group
1271 Avenue of the Americas, New York, NY 10020
Visit our Web site at www.twbookmark.com

First Edition: February 2006

Library of Congress Cataloging-in-Publication Data
Cox, Anna-Lisa.
  A stronger kinship : one town's extraordinary story of hope and faith / Anna-Lisa Cox.
    p.   cm.
  ISBN 10: 0-316-11018-3
  ISBN 13: 978-0-316-11018-1
  1. African Americans — Michigan — Covert (Township) — Attitudes.   2. Whites —
Michigan — Covert (Township) — Attitudes.   3. Covert (Mich. : Township) —
History — 19th century.   4. Covert (Mich. : Township) — Race relations —
History — 19th century.   I. Title.
F574.C73C69 2006
305.896'073077413 — dc22   2005020332

10   9   8   7   6   5   4   3   2   1

Q-MART

Book design by Jo Anne Metsch

Printed in the United States of America

To my parents, Karen and John,

for showing me the way

Contents

Cast of Characters

William Frank Conner

Born in North Carolina in 1838. Came to Michigan in the early 1850s with his parents, William Bright and Elizabeth (Schrugs) Conner, his extended family, as well as Himebrick Tyler. Joined the Michigan First Colored Regiment, also known as the 102nd USCT, in 1863. Came to Covert in 1866 with his extended family, where he became a successful and wealthy farmer. Won numerous political positions in Covert, including Justice of the Peace, making him the first black man to hold that position in Michigan. Was one of the founders of Covert's Emancipation festival. Died in 1908.
Wife: Elizabeth Ann Shepard
Children: John L. ("Johnny"), Letticia, Clara, Myrtie*

Nancy (Conner) Seaton

Born in North Carolina in 1845. Sister to William Frank Conner. When her husband returned from the Civil War they moved to Covert with her parents, brother, and extended family. Nancy and her husband moved briefly to Lawrence, Kansas, in 1871 and returned to Covert in 1872. Nancy died sometime during the 1930s after moving to Lansing, Michigan, in the 1920s.
Husband: Joseph Seaton
Children: Joseph, Emmaline ("Emma"), Ora

Himebrick Tyler

Born in 1833 in North Carolina. Came with the Conners to Michigan in the early 1850s. Joined the Michigan First Regiment with his brother and father-in-law in 1863. Moved with them to Covert after the war.

First wife: Zylphia Conner
Himebrick and Zylphia's children: Cornelius, Octavius, and James
Second wife: Louisa Mathews (widow, formally married to Allison Mathews, who died during the Civil War)
Louisa's children: Isadore, Mary Jane, Allison
Himebrick and Louisa's children: Almira, Alvin Sheridan, Julia Ann, Elvira, Arvena, Sherman Emery (In the mid 1890s Sheridan would be involved in a legal case that would go all the way to the Michigan Supreme Court.)

William Bright Conner

Born in North Carolina in 1812. Was a successful owner of a turpentine plantation in Greene County, North Carolina, before leaving the state for the North in the early 1850s. He died in 1901.

First wife: Elizabeth Schrugs (died before they moved to Covert)
William Bright and Elizabeth's children: Franklin, William Frank, Nancy, John, Zylphia
Second wife: Abigail
William Bright and Abigail's children: William Frank, Alexander, Theodore, Allen, Frederick Douglass, Sarah, Ulysses

Henry Shepard

Born into slavery around 1817 in Virginia and taken into Kentucky as a child. In his early twenties he fled bondage twice, succeeding the second time in getting to Canada. Returned to the United States shortly thereafter and settled in Cass County, Michigan. Henry was a successful farmer in Cass County and began a secret career as a conductor on the Underground Railroad. Although he was in his forties when the Civil War broke out, he enlisted in the Michigan First Colored Regiment, along with his son-in-law William Frank Conner. Henry and his wife moved to Covert in 1877. Henry died in 1884.

Wife: Martha Barton

Children: Henry and Martha had fifteen children, six of whom survived into adulthood, including Nancy, who would marry William Frank Conner and later persuade her parents to move to Covert.

Alfred Packard

Born in 1834 in New York. Came to Covert in 1868 from Ohio, where his family had been living for some time. He started the first successful logging and milling business in Covert. Nephew to William Packard, who with his sons (including William O. Packard) would join with Alfred in building three large mills in Covert, bringing a logging boom to the area. Before coming to Covert both Alfred and William Sr. had been active in their Congregational church in Chatham, Ohio, where they had been followers of a radically abolitionist minister. Once in Covert the Packard family was aggressive in its policies to hire an integrated workforce and recruit African American congregants to the Covert Congregational Church.

Dawson Pompey

Born between 1801 and 1804, birthplace unknown. By 1850 he was living in Indiana with his brother, Fielding, and their families. Two of his sons, Napoleon and Washington, came to Covert in 1866 and soon persuaded their father to join them. He was the first black man elected to political office in Covert, in 1868 (illegally).

First wife: Sina

Dawson and Sina's children: Eliza, Lorenzo, Napoleon, Washington, Catherine, Susan, Dawson Jr., Elias
Second wife: Hulda
Dawson and Hulda's children: Sylvester, Grace

Frank Rood

Born in Michigan in 1864, Frank Rood grew up in Covert. The Rood family was distantly related to the Packards, who had also originated in Plainfield, Massachusetts.
Parents: Edward and Flora (came from Plainfield to Michigan around 1864)
Frank's uncles in Covert: Thaddeus Rood (moved to Covert in 1869), David Rood (retired to Covert in the 1880s after decades of missionary work in Africa)

*All children mentioned are only those that survived into adulthood.

Plat map of Covert Township, Michigan, 1873. At the time, Covert was still called Deerfield. *Deerfield* was such a popular community name in that region of Michigan that the post office asked the residents to change their town's name. In the mid-1870s William Packard successfully petitioned the Michigan state senate to change the name to Covert.

D.J. Lake, *Atlas of Van Buren County, Michigan* (Philadelphia: C.O. Titus, 1873)

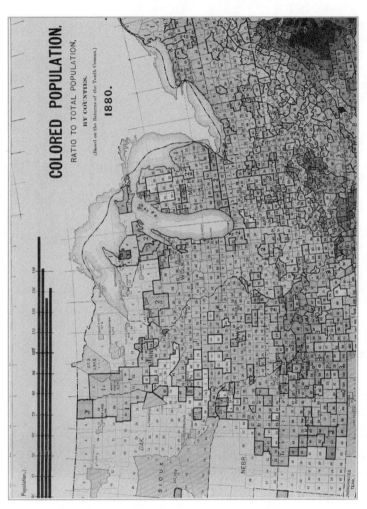

The Midwest's African American population to the county level. Covert is in Van Buren County, which is in southern Michigan along Lake Michigan, where there is a large number 3 on the map. At the time Van Buren County had a black population of 2 to 10 percent.
Plate 24: Population ("Colored Population"), Fletcher Hewes and Henry Gannett, *Scribner's Statistical Atlas of the United States* (New York: C. Scribner's Sons, 1883). Library of Congress Geography and Map Division, Washington, D.C.

A STRONGER KINSHIP

Introduction

"The differences between black folk and white folk are not blood or color, and the ties that bind us are deeper than those that separate us. The common road of hope which we all have traveled has brought us into a stronger kinship than any words, laws, or legal claims."

— Richard Wright,
12 Million Black Voices[1]

In the heartland of nineteenth-century America, a mixed-race community existed where blacks and whites lived as equal citizens. Starting in the 1860s the people of this place broke both laws and social expectations to develop a community of radical equality. Schools and churches were completely integrated, blacks and whites married, and power and wealth were shared between the races. Together, over the next fifty years, these residents of Covert, Michigan, continued to shatter the legal and social barriers to black freedom. This book is their story, a story that stretches across the decades from the Civil War to the close of the nineteenth century.

In many ways the period in which Covert was founded, just

before and after the Civil War, was similar to the turbulent years of the 1960s. White Americans were called on to vote for sweeping civil rights bills that, for the first time in our nation's history, made black people citizens. As the century passed, many outside of Covert lost sight of the dream of equality. A number of the abolitionist communities that had been settled throughout the Midwest before the Civil War lost their direction and drive after the end of slavery, and many of them ended up disbanding or disappearing. The backlash against the radical changes of the Civil War era was not swift, but it was sure. As the years rolled down toward the end of the century, civil rights were slowly worn away. In 1896 they were dealt a crushing blow by the infamous Supreme Court decision *Plessy v. Ferguson*, which legalized segregation and opened the floodgates to institutional, legal, and social racism.

The citizens of Covert were well aware of the shameful events that were occurring all around them, even in the Midwest, but they made decision after decision to create an integrated community. This, in a region made up of small close-knit communities that were often intolerant of, if not outright hostile to, difference. This, in a region where ethnic and racial minorities had to keep to themselves to survive. This, in a time when the rest of the nation slid into the maw of Jim Crow.

In 1939, when Jim Crow was still dismembering America's race relations in its murderous jaws, Richard Wright, the influential African American author of such works as *Native Son* and *Black Boy*, wrote in all too apparent agony, "We cannot fight back; we have no arms; we cannot vote; and the law is white. There are no black policemen, black Justices of the Peace . . . or black men anywhere in the government."[2] Little did he know that sixty-four years earlier Covert's mainly white electorate had voted a young black man into the position of Justice of the Peace to lead an integrated group of constables.

This one community's history testifies that despite our nation's history of violence, hate, and injustice, there was a place where ordinary black and white Americans treated each other as equals and as friends. Covert was not a theoretical utopia; it was a very human community. Its residents were not perfect people, they did not all have the same reasons for their radical attitudes and actions, nor were they color-blind. Knowing it was impossible to ignore difference, they recognized it — in some cases even celebrated it. Many of them held a shared belief in the ideals of integration and equality, and they did not let race become a reason to denigrate or be denigrated.

Those who created Covert were not naive Midwesterners, sheltered in the heart of the heartland, unaware of the world beyond their county line, being good because they knew no other way to be. The people who settled Covert in the 1860s were well-traveled, out to claim what was then a wilderness frontier. And those who followed them in the later years, when Covert had become a more settled farming community, were travelers seeking opportunities to live as they saw best. They came from all over the nation and the world, and none were untouched by the turmoil of racial politics that swirled around that era. Remarkably, the people of Covert were able to preserve and pass on their ideology of a community of equality through the generations and to new residents. Their culture survived through the bonds created between individuals, families, business partners, church members, and friends.

True, they were a small community, no more than seventeen hundred by the 1890s, and blacks made up only about 8 percent of the township's population. That was, however, a large percentage for the Midwest, where blacks were rare and often hated with that odd Midwestern racism that was not based on numbers and could be touched off by the presence of only one black person, or none at all.

Covert was not perfect, and it faced internal social and economic upheavals that could have destroyed the bonds between the races there. There was the logging boom of the 1870s that more than doubled the township's population. The new residents, both black and white, had little knowledge of the unusual nature of race relations in Covert, and a potentially explosive situation was created by newcomers streaming into the community just as the more settled black residents in Covert were making their most aggressive bids for power and recognition. Then the logging boom died at the same time that the nation was hit by its worst depression thus far, leaving Covert's economy in shambles. When the depression was at its worst, a suit brought by a black Covert resident against a white Covert resident would openly pit the races against each other. But even in a time of economic insecurity, Covert's residents continued to hold fast to the bonds they had created.

The successes that people of African descent experienced in Covert were not a matter of a paternalistic white community allowing the blacks in their midst to be granted some power. Rather, it was blacks who constantly required and demanded power and recognition. Their actions made it clear that they saw themselves as citizens of the nation and deserving of all the rights of a citizen. They had fought for their country, they had helped to settle it on many frontiers, and they had shaped its identity.

Not only did they demand equality, they also demanded recognition. Covert may have been integrated, but by the late 1870s, its black residents created an annual Emancipation festival that celebrated their distinctive identity. The Emancipation festivals were not only a way for the African Americans to make their presence known within the community but were also a way of symbolizing what they saw as their essential selves.[3] Through the festivities they were making clear that they were both of the community of Covert and of the community of the United States, sharing its past experiences and memories, as well as owning their own unique heritage and memories.

So why has Covert's story never been told before? Covert never tried to hide its history. Unlike Cass County and other African American communities in the Midwest before the Civil War, it did not have to cloak its radical and integrated identity. Covert's pioneers tried very hard to make integration and equality a norm, but they may have been fated by their very success to remain little known in history. They made that norm so — well, so normal — that later generations may well have thought that there was nothing special to report about their community. It was home, a small rural community in the middle of the Midwest — what was so remarkable about that? They may have also been doomed by their location —

the rural Midwest. What was once the frontier and a hotbed of racial revolution was, by the late twentieth century, perceived as a locale where race had little place.

Of course, Covert and the very few communities like it were not typical. While Covert was flourishing, elsewhere racism was rampant, with mob violence rising to a level of warfare even in the Midwest. Within a nation where race relations were corrupted by hatred, fear, and despair, the people of Covert created their kinship and community. So this is the story of another America, a tale both of what was and what could have been. This small community of farming folk daily made their brave choices to love instead of hate, trust instead of fear, and hope instead of despair, even as the storm of racism rose round them. That raging storm left a wreckage of grief, mistrust, and anger in its wake. Yet Covert's residents stood firm against that fury. Their community was a shelter from the storm, and today Covert's story still offers a haven for hope. This history was almost lost: for stories of peace, trust, love, and hope are often quieter stories than those the storm brings, but Covert's story is one that is as moving, powerful, and great as any storm. Covert is a testament that through great courage and good faith, people can stand against the storm and create something new and fine, together.

Chapter 1

The Bleeding Heartland

"The prejudice against color which exists in this country is sinful in the sight of God, and should be immediately repented of."

—Excerpt from a Midwestern
Anti-Slavery Society constitution,[1] 1841

Michigan, in the middle of the 1850s, in the middle of the century, in the middle of the nation, in the middle of a crisis that would soon tear it apart.

Today the heartland is perceived as a vast flat landscape that holds little interest for those living on the coasts, but in the mid 1850s, it was the focus of the nation; it was where the United States was literally creating itself. The Midwest was perceived as a promised land by Europeans, Yankees, and Southerners of all races. But what that promise led to was deep disagreement, and by the time Covert was founded, in 1855, the heartland it belonged to was wounded and bleeding. Soon blood would be spilled in the very capital itself. In May of 1856 United States Senator Charles Sumner, in the midst of a passionate speech against the violence being perpetrated by pro-slavery forces in Kansas, was physically attacked by an enraged South Carolina congressman, Preston Brooks, who bludgeoned Sumner with his cane so fiercely that Sumner's body was left broken on the Senate floor, close to death.

Kansas was not the only Midwestern state to consider slavery. Although the Northwest Ordinance of 1787 officially made slavery illegal in the Northwest Territories, there were many loopholes allowing current slaveholders many rights, loopholes that, for all intents and purposes, kept slavery alive in the Northwest Territories until those territories became states. William Henry Harrison, the governor of what was in 1801 called the Indiana Territory, was open about his desire to officially bring back slavery to the region he reigned over, and statehood did not change the opinions of many fellow Midwesterners regarding the status of black Americans.[2] Just as in the Eastern states such as New York, there was no immediate end to the practice of human bondage in the Midwest; instead, it was a slow and gradual process allowing slave owners to get the full "worth" out of the young slaves they had just bought that kept the practice alive. Those Old Northwest–Territory states — such as Indiana, Ohio, Illinois, Michigan, and Wisconsin — had to finally give up any hopes of slavery if they wanted to achieve statehood, but this did not mean that things were decided. Michigan, despite its large number of New England settlers, had been the last to relinquish its ties to slavery when it achieved statehood, in 1837. But this was not all that surprising, for such common loopholes meant that people were enslaved and under a master's command in New York in the late 1830s.[3] Although today many think of slavery as being exclusively associated with the South and large plantations, slaves worked and survived all over the United States, and slavery existed in one form or another in the North until the late 1840s.[4] Importation of slaves was officially barred in the United States in 1808, but illegal importation continued all along the coast, from New England to South Carolina. More than thirty years later, President Martin Van Buren tried his best to strengthen the law against the importation of slaves, but in 1841 his successor, President John Tyler, bemoaned the fact that, if anything, the slave trade in the United States was increasing. Slave breeding was well accepted by the end of the eighteenth century, and plantation owners boasted to their friends of the particular fertility of certain slave women, even giving bonuses to those who had the most children. As one plantation owner delightedly admitted of the children born into his ownership, "Every one of them . . . was worth two hundred dollars . . . the moment it drew breath."[5] Not surprisingly, slave families were torn apart when economics took precedence over their owners' respect for kin ties. Some states, such as Louisiana, passed laws forbidding slave owners to sell children until they reached the age of ten, while other states tried to keep the practice from becoming too common, but it was all too heart-wrenchingly real.[6] No matter how loving some owners might have been, they were also farmers, and farmers were prone to bankruptcy and all the fluctuations of the market that farmers have always been vulnerable to, and when such disasters struck, all valuable goods in the ownership of the farmer had to be sold. Sojourner Truth, who would later become the great anti-slavery and feminist orator, lost all of her brothers and sisters to sale even though they were hundreds of miles from the South, living enslaved in New York. At the age of nine, Sojourner herself was sold, her heartbroken and devastated parents witnessing their last child being taken away from them. Later she felt the same pain her parents had suffered when her six-year-old son was sold to someone in Alabama. She fought his sale in the courts and had him returned to her, but it took a year, and by that time his tiny body was horrifically battered from the beatings he had endured.[7]

It was a terrible life. While stories of cruel masters were claimed as rarities by slavery supporters, the advertisements slave owners printed when their chattel escaped gave lie to their claim, for the vast majority of such announcements described the unique and terrible scars or even fresh wounds that the escaped carried on their bodies as testimony to the brutality of their treatment.[8] Even Thomas Jefferson — himself a slave owner and deeply conflicted over slavery and the role of people from Africa in America — wrote, "The whole commerce between master and slave is a perpetual exercise of the most boisterous passions. . . . The most unremitting despotism on the one part, and degrading submissions on the other." He was aware that this was a system that corrupted both the enslaved and the enslaver, a system that he saw, at the very dawn of the nineteenth century, as perpetuating its poisonous culture down through the generations. As he noted, "Our children see this, and learn to imitate it. The parents storm, the child looks on . . . and thus [they are] nursed, educated, and daily exercised in tyranny."9

Some of the largest plantations were in South Carolina, where great riches were created from the dank and dreadful work of growing rice. The swamps and lowlands so ideal for rice cultivation harbored snakes and alligators, although those might be deemed friendly when compared with the numerous deadly diseases rampant in the rank waters. Slave owners built majestic and beautiful homes and grounds, sometimes over-looking their vast watery domains. These plantation owners prided themselves on their paternal benevolence toward the human beings they owned. Those they owned had little chance to let their true feelings be known about their plight except by running away.

Although the popular vision of slavery is one of many slaves bending low over epic fields of cotton bushes, only a quarter of the almost four million people enslaved in the United States by 1860 were living on plantations that owned more than fifty slaves.10

Slaves working on small farms in the up-country South might have had the companionship of only one or two other slaves, a pattern very similar to rural slavery in the North in the early nineteenth century. There were urban slaves who were often highly skilled and worked in smaller groups, with much more contact with others, both slave and free.

Nevertheless, by 1855, much of what was considered the civilized portion of the nation, whether North or South, was deeply enmeshed in the plantation economy. Rice, sugar, tobacco, and cotton were cultivated by slaves in the South, while the North wove the cotton into cloth in its many mills, smoked the tobacco, sweetened its coffee and cakes with the sugar, ate and exported the rice. Meanwhile the South was hungry for the North's technology, buying machines ranging from cotton gins to plows, and was happy to borrow from Northern investors, hold money in Northern banks, and send its sons to Northern schools.

From the earliest days of the nation, there had been those passionate in their belief that the United States should allow freedom and equality for all, but by 1855 the efforts of many were forcing the nation to realize that this was an issue that had to be dealt with. Those who organized to end human enslavement in America called themselves abolitionists. Sojourner Truth, Frederick Douglass, David Walker, George Moses Horton, Robert Purvis, Samuel Cornish, and Sarah Parker Redmond are just a few of the many who forced the issue. They and their white counterparts, including William Lloyd Garrison, Benjamin Lundy, Lydia Maria Child, Arthur Tappan, Lucretia Mott, and Henry Ward Beecher, organized important abolitionist groups and traveled throughout the North giving speeches and publishing important texts that moved many to their cause. There were also the foot soldiers, those who gave few speeches but through actions freed many long before the war freed all. Starting in the 1770s many Quakers in the South had renounced slavery and begun freeing their slaves. By the early nineteenth century, the Quakers had begun to move north, often to the Midwest, in order to create communities of freedom for all.

Although anti-slavery and pro-slavery advocates spoke as if there were only a North and a South, sometimes it seemed that there was only the United States and the frontier, and in 1855 the frontier was the Midwest. The battle over whether the nation should be slave or free raged fiercely there. Those in the North who wished to actively fight slavery moved in great numbers to Ohio, Michigan, Illinois, Indiana, and Iowa, often encamping themselves along the rough and porous border between slavery and freedom. Their many stories of struggle, and the people they helped to free, have often been erased by the great flood of war that was soon to be unleashed upon the land, but these settlers were the first of the fighters for freedom for all races.

Soon other abolitionists began moving to the Midwestern frontier in the hopes that there they could create a new way of being. John Shipherd, one of the founders of the radical abolitionist community of Oberlin, which would produce Oberlin College, chose to relocate to Ohio from Vermont because he saw the Midwest as a place in which to create a culture that could improve "our nation and the empires of the earth."[11] He thought of the Midwest as the heartland, but in a more metaphysical sense than the phrase is used today: Shipherd's heartland was one of radical, and for him Christian, principles that insisted love was without bounds and all races and genders could live in equality and harmony.[12] Others started colleges that would follow in his integrationist path, including Antioch and Otterbein, but John Shipherd and the Oberlin abolitionists were some of the first to act on their beliefs. While the first African American men began receiving their

BAs from New England colleges in the mid 1820s, Oberlin was the first to grant an African American woman a BA, in 1862.[13] Shipherd's vision, and his college, would ultimately split the Presbyterian church asunder, a schism that proved to be a foreshadowing of what would occur in his nation.[14]

Numerous other small rural abolitionist communities were created throughout the Midwest during this time, including Wayne County, Indiana; New Athens, Ohio; Denmark and Salem, Iowa — to name just a few. Free African American settlements also grew up under or near the protection of Quaker and Congregational abolitionists, such as in Cass County, Michigan; the Beech and Roberts settlements in Indiana; and a myriad of others in Iowa, Wisconsin, Ohio, and Illinois. Others were founded strictly by people of African descent, such as New Philadelphia, Illinois; Brooklyn, Illinois; Westfield Township, Iowa; and Nicodemus, Kansas.[15]

Some of these communities, such as Oberlin, could be considered "utopian" — settlements deliberately created to make an ideal a reality. The first half of the nineteenth century saw a flourishing of such communities, from those based on new religions to those that turned their back on faith in anything but individualism. Covert was not utopian, but that did not mean that the radical racial realities that occurred there were not also held by classically utopian communities. North Elba, New York, probably came the closest to matching Covert. The ardent abolitionist Gerrit Smith gave thousands of acres to blacks in upstate New York toward his vision of a society where blacks and whites could live together in freedom. One of its most famous settlers, strongly pro-integrationist John

Brown, made a point of befriending his black neighbors, often shocking his white visitors by seating them at the same table with his black guests. Although he later moved to Kansas, where he became famous for his exploits, his heart was in North Elba, where he would be buried. Unfortunately, like most utopian communities, North Elba did not exist for long. Few of the whites John Brown knew were willing to share in his integrationist vision.[16]

While abolitionist communities flourished, they were often embattled, for their very existence was an affront to pro-slavery supporters and white supremacists, who were also settling throughout the Midwest. Nevertheless, it was abolitionist communities like these that helped make possible the Underground Railroad (a series of shelters and safe homes that slaves could use to travel North undetected) and sometimes encouraged black settlement in the Midwest. Because many of those slaves who escaped made their way to Canada or refused to have themselves tallied in any federal census, their numbers are difficult to track. Slave owners in the South and abolitionists in the North alike had every reason to exaggerate the numbers of those escaping, but there is good reason to believe that around a hundred thousand traveled themselves free.[17] Operating the Underground Railroad was a dangerous business. By 1850 a new, harsher version of the Fugitive Slave Act was passed that punished anyone who aided a person who was trying to gain freedom. These communities of abolitionists and blacks in the Midwest were now battlegrounds, for the lines were no longer along the borders between the slave and free states but as far as the slave raiders cared to travel.

Recapturing "lost" slaves was a lucrative business, for slaves were of immense value. Whites would take out mortgages in order to own one, and by the 1850s owning a slave in the South was the equivalent of owning a piece of the American Dream. In reality only about a quarter of the Southern population owned slaves by 1860, but for many of the non-slave-owning Southerners, becoming a slave owner was a sign of success. No wonder so many Southern whites were willing to break away from their nation and fight for their state's right to continue to hold people in bondage, for they were eager to preserve the promise that someday they too could become slave owners and enjoy the status that position entailed.[18] If human property was "lost," those who owned it would often offer high rewards for its return. These rewards bred hunters who were willing to go to great lengths to capture their human prey. Escaped slaves recaptured were often beaten, tortured, or maimed to terrify the other enslaved people around them who dreamed of freedom.

One such slave hunter went traveling through Ohio and Indiana to find abolitionist communities that might be harboring people he believed were chattel. Disguising himself as an abolitionist lecturer, he successfully sniffed out a number of his quarry, who were promptly taken back into slavery.[19] Others were much bolder. Cass County, Michigan, had long been known to be home to a large community of African Americans, many of whom had been slaves before they left the South. The slave raiders must have envisioned a gold mine awaiting them there, so they rode North armed as if for war, with guns, ropes, and horses to capture and carry away as many as they could. When they arrived in Cass County, they must have been amazed. The township of Cassopolis alone had more than six hundred black residents, and the invaders were met with ferocious resistance from both blacks and whites.[20] (It is difficult to know what must have been more surprising, the whites who were willing to risk their lives for their black neighbors or the black people themselves, who rose up like the bravest soldiers to protect their kin and kind.) The slavers ended up taking their case to the courts.[21] The abolitionists who had chosen to resist the raid paid a terrible toll, for the courts fined the Quakers of Cass County outrageous sums for helping their friends.[22]

In direct opposition to the slave raiders were the conductors — male and female, black and white — who rarely came armed with anything but their courage and who traveled into the South to aid those refugees from slavery. Harriet Tubman is probably one of the most famous of these conductors, and justly so. Unlike many of the white conductors, she placed herself in terrible danger every time she went into the South, for as an escaped slave she would have been considered lost property found if she were ever discovered. Although she protected the people she helped conduct by rarely talking of how many she had led to freedom, it is known that she traveled into the slave lands almost twenty times, walking at least three hundred slaves to freedom.[23]

White conductors had an advantage in that they could travel through the South freely, although they still risked great danger in getting people out of the slave states. Calvin Fairbanks, a famous conductor, ended up imprisoned for years, but before his capture he had helped many people into the North. He used numerous techniques, but one of the most ingenious he devised with a friend, Miss Webster, who posed as a teacher traveling with her chaperon and three of her slaves, who were in reality Fairbanks and three escapees.[24]

For sheer audacity and imagination, John Fairfield had all the other white conductors beat. Fairfield had been raised in Virginia as the son of a slaveholder, but as he reached adulthood, he could no longer stand to live surrounded by a system that, though he had been raised within it, seemed barbaric and cruel. He decided to move North but took with him a friend who happened to be an enslaved black man. He was successfully able to flee the South with his friend, and emboldened by his triumph, Fairfield turned into one of the most successful conductors of all time. He was deeply familiar with all the ways and customs of the slave South, as well as bearing the correct accent for the region, and his ingenuity was astounding. He started bringing out only a few at a time, often pretending that they were his personal retinue. But in time he became bolder, traveling with up to fifteen slaves while disguised as a slave trader. One of his most extraordinary acts was to help twenty-eight slaves escape a plantation by convincing the whites around him that they were part of a funeral procession. Fairfield and his charges would often emerge in southern Indiana at the home of Levi Coffin, a Quaker who had personally helped more than three thousand escaping slaves, and there he would leave the people he had led out of states as far south as Louisiana and plunge back across the border to continue his aid. Just as it was with all conductors, every time Fairbanks left for the South, his friends feared they would never see him again. In 1860 those fears were realized when he did not return. Some time later reports came to them that he had been shot.[25]

While many slaves were assisted by these conductors, uncounted numbers took their courage in their own hands and, rebelling against the idea that they were property, ran. When they did run, it was often the abolitionist communities across the Midwest that either helped them farther North or gave them a place to call home.

Slavery was a terrible system, yet many historians believe that it did not always entirely dehumanize or destroy slaves, who managed through various means of resistance to keep aspects of their culture, kinship, and courage alive.[26] Despite extraordinary difficulties, a substantial number of people enslaved in America still managed, against great odds, to have families and keep blood ties, and even facing the dangers of escaping, they bravely did all they could to keep together as kin.

One such slave was John Walker, and the community that aided him was Salem, Iowa. Salem had been founded by abolitionist Quakers close to the Missouri border. They made their community and homes open to slaves fleeing from Missouri and other slave states and often helped them to get to Canada, where they could be safe from those hunting them. In June of 1848 John Walker left the safety of Salem, which had harbored him in the months after his escape, and returned to Missouri to the farm of his old master, Ruel Daggs, who still held Walker's wife and children enslaved.[27]

Walker made it all the way back to Daggs's farm, in Luray, Missouri, without being spotted or captured and there found his beloved wife, Mary, and his children. Mary had probably given up hope that she would ever see her husband alive, and their reunion must have been sweet. Mary and John made the risky decision that in addition to escaping with their young children, they would also take fellow slave Sam Fulcher and his family, and one other slave as well, a teenager named Julia.

Under the cover of darkness, the group made it to the farmstead of a sympathetic white farmer by the name of Richard Liggon, who was willing to risk the wrath of his neighbors as well as the harsh legal consequences of harboring fugitive slaves in Missouri. In a heavy summer storm, Liggon drove the escaping family and their friends to the Des Moines River. There they boarded a makeshift raft that barely got them to the other shore in safety. Once they were safe on the Iowa side, they waited in the rain for their Quaker friends to come from Salem and take them home.

But they were not free of danger yet. Daggs, his sons William and George, and their friend James McClure went straight into Iowa, suspecting that their property would head to Salem. Once in Iowa they found an aid in the form of Samuel Slaughter, a farmer who had recently come from Virginia. For a share in the reward money that Daggs was offering, Slaughter agreed to help him recapture the people who had fled slavery and return them to bondage. Daggs then went home across the border to keep an eye on the rest of his slaves.

The fierce summer storms continued, with heavy rain turning the dark soil into difficult mud, hampering the pursuers.

But when the rain ended on Sunday, so did the escaping slaves' luck, for the wet earth plainly revealed to the trackers the marks of a wagon leading from the river to Salem. The trackers spurred their horses in pursuit, and the wagon was soon in sight, but then it began to gain speed, and the chase was on. The wagon barreled through the Iowa muck, trying to make it to Salem as the pursuers were gaining. All of a sudden Slaughter and McClure saw the wagon careening off the track into the woods, where it disappeared. Spurring their horses harder, they followed the tracks until they came to the wagon, stopped in the middle of the woods, the horses panting in exhaustion.

But all that was inside were three young white men, who boldly informed the slave catchers that they had never heard of any escaping slaves and were merely returning from a fishing trip. The young men then must have asked their pursuers why they had been chasing them, to which Slaughter replied that they were searching for two stolen horses, and theirs had looked familiar. The pursuers went with the young men into Salem and tried looking there for their quarry, but no one was willing to help them, and they had no success.

They stayed Sunday night in Salem, but Monday they returned secretly to the woods, where they found the escaped group. John Walker desperately tried to fight them off but was beaten badly and tied to a horse. Slaughter left McClure with the heartbroken and terrified group while he headed into Salem in hopes of hiring men to help him bring his bounty back to Missouri. Not surprisingly, he was unsuccessful, and when he returned he found McClure and the fugitives surrounded by more than a dozen men from Salem, who made it clear that McClure and Slaughter would not be able to take their human bounty away. One member of the group said he was "willing to wade through Missouri blood" in order to keep the fugitives safe in Iowa.[28]

A rather heated argument then took place, but the crowd was growing larger, and it soon became clear to Slaughter and McClure that this was a debate they were going to lose. They agreed to go to Salem's Justice of the Peace to try to settle the dispute. On the walk there Slaughter, determined not to let Walker escape, trod alongside him with a hard grip on Walker's arm. Seeing this, a Salem man pulled Walker free and told him to punch Slaughter the next time Slaughter tried to hold him. Loose, Walker made a dash through the crowd to freedom, and the Salem residents closed around Slaughter, preventing him from pursuing Walker. Walker's wife, Mary, seeing her husband's actions, began to complain loudly that she was too tired to walk anymore. Sam Fulcher persuaded Slaughter to let the women stay behind and rest their too weary selves by telling Slaughter that he would sacrifice himself and return to Missouri.

Those who continued arrived at the home of the Justice of the Peace, who questioned Slaughter and McClure. When they told him what their mission was, the Justice of the Peace asked them if they had any written proof from the slave owner that they were there to find his slaves. Slaughter and McClure admitted that they did not. With what must have been a triumphant flourish, the Justice of the Peace pulled out a copy of *The Revised Statutes of the Territory of Iowa* and read aloud this passage: "If any person or persons shall forcibly steal, take, or arrest any man woman or child in this Territory . . . with a design to take him or her out of this territory without having legally established his, her, or their claim according to the laws of this territory, or of the United States, shall upon conviction thereof, be punished by a fine not exceeding one thousand dollars and by imprisonment in the penitentiary at hard labor not exceeding ten years."[29] A thousand dollars was a terrifyingly high amount of money in that cash-poor society, and ten years' hard labor is unattractive in any century. Not aware that the Supreme Court had decided that this law was unconstitutional, and surrounded by an angry group of abolitionists, Slaughter and McClure gave in and left, to the cheers of the residents of Salem.

Unfortunately, the story does not end here. John Walker lived free with his wife and family, and Sam Fulcher and his son also managed to disappear into the freedom of the North. However, Fulcher's wife and the young Julia were eventually recaptured and sent back to Daggs. Although popular legend has it that they too managed to escape to Canada, all too likely they were condemned to live in bondage, far from their loved ones, until Missouri decided to finally free its slaves, fifteen years later. [30]

During all this, in the nation's capital a new political party was struggling into existence. Some members of this new entity called themselves Free-Soilers (although made up of some strongly abolitionist members, most were just anti-slavery, seeing black slave laborers as competing against free labor, which was most often defined as the legitimate right of whites only);

others had been members of the short-lived but very popular Know-Nothing Party, which was rabidly xenophobic; while still others had been part of the once powerful but now disbanded old Whig party. There were even some Democrats in this new party's ranks who were breaking away from their now Southern-dominated party. All of these men (and they were all men, for women would not gain the vote until almost three-quarters of a century had passed) called themselves Republicans.

The members of this new Republican Party had different goals and aims, some overtly discriminatory, for many Know-Nothings were anti-Catholic and deeply distrustful of the Irish immigrants who had been fleeing the potato famine. Most in the newly formed Republican Party were not interested in freeing the slaves, just intent on not allowing people of African descent, slave or free, to flood into what they considered to be their portions of the nation. Some few members of this new party did believe that all slaves should be free and equal, but they were a distinct minority.

What united almost all the Republicans was their opposition to the Kansas-Nebraska Act, which had effectively negated the Missouri Compromise. The Missouri Compromise had been passed in 1820 in response to Missouri's desire to become a state. There were already a number of people being held enslaved in the Missouri Territory, and many Southerners in Congress called for it to be formed as a slave state. If Missouri became a slave state, however, the balance between slave and free states would go to the slaveholders' advantage. The compromise reached could easily have been called the Maine Compromise, for Maine was created from a portion of Massachusetts and declared a free state. There were other important factors in the compromise, most notably, that any state past a certain northerly latitude formed thereafter had to be a free state, with the implicit assumption that any states created below that line could be slave states. Slave owners gained one final advantage out of this compromise: any of their human chattel that managed to escape to freedom in a free region were not free but were still chattel and could be hunted down and returned to bondage. Senator Stephen Douglas, an Illinois Democrat who would one day pit his oratory powers against Lincoln, urged those in Washington to, if not break the Missouri Compromise, then bend it to the limit by allowing Kansas and Nebraska, both states far north of the line drawn by the Missouri Compromise, to have the option of becoming slave states. Douglas, deeply interested in the development of the regions west of Chicago, was determined to have Nebraska and Kansas become states and, even though he claimed abolitionist sympathies, was willing to work with Southern slaveholders to gain his goal. Soon he had pushed through the Kansas-Nebraska Act with the caveat that those living in Kansas and Nebraska could decide for themselves which way their new state should proceed. Far from being seen as a states' rights issue, as Douglas had hoped, this act was seen as a clear break with the Missouri Compromise, and it quickly whipped up the North's wrath. Worse yet, the invitation to Kansas and Nebraska to choose their own fates meant that those who felt strongly about whether those states should be slave or free moved to the region as quickly as they could, causing violence that bordered on war there. Kansas, in particular, became a battlefield as abolitionist and pro-slavery supporters, often heavily armed, flooded into the region. After months of violence the community of Lawrence was attacked by a pro-slavery mob that managed to destroy a goodly portion of the town. The militant abolitionist John Brown, who was raised in Ohio, was enraged by the violence being done against abolitionists in Lawrence and gathered a group of like-minded followers and attacked a pro-slavery settlement at Pottawatomie Creek, killing five of its residents.

Kansas was not the only state to see blood shed over the issue of slavery. For years there had been clashes between the races as well as between pro- and anti-slavery supporters across the Midwest. One of the most infamous was the killing of the Presbyterian minister Elijah Lovejoy. Lovejoy had started as a minister at a church in St. Louis, Missouri, but when he dared to speak out against the horrifying killing of a slave who was burned at the stake, he was forced to leave his position and the city. He moved to Alton, Illinois, and there became minister of a Presbyterian church as well as the publisher of a strongly abolitionist newspaper. Lovejoy's press was attacked and destroyed by angry pro-slavery mobs a number of times. Finally, on the night of November 7, 1837, he was attacked trying to defend his press from yet another mob, which turned deadly and murdered him.[31]

This was the Midwest that saw the birth of Covert, Michigan.

More than likely the Yankees who settled Covert in 1855 had little thought that issues of race, freedom, and equality that were currently convulsing their nation would soon become an intimate part of their lives. Instead, they seemed more intent on celebrating the past. In a move seemingly done to deliberately confuse future historians, the Yankee settlers of Covert first named their community Deerfield. The original American Deerfield, first settled as a Puritan outpost in late-seventeenth-century Massachusetts, was the site of the infamous Deerfield Massacre of the early eighteenth century, when French-allied Indians attacked and killed many of the residents.[32] Yankees arriving in southwestern Michigan may well have thought of themselves as similar to those embattled settlers. Here they were, perceiving themselves to be of Puritan stock, settling in an area the French had controlled for almost two centuries which was still peopled by Indians who had been converted by the French to Catholicism. No wonder, then, that they — and other communities near them — all decided to call their communities by the same name. Eventually, the United States Postal Service begged some of these southwestern Michigan Deerfields to change their names to spare the postal service confusion, and in 1876, William O. Packard, then a state senator, had the name of one of these Deerfields officially changed to Covert.[33]

But of course, "covert" meant something very specific and very relevant. The word connotes concealment and shelter. This community was a symbol of all that white supremacists were arguing was impossible and overtly abhorred. Given the state of things in the rest of the nation, a humble pride would certainly be understandable among this community of equals. These settlers of Covert were people of great faith and were almost certainly aware of this passage from the book of Isaiah: "There shall be a tabernacle for a shadow in the day time from the heat, and for a place of refuge, and for a covert from storm and from rain" (4:6). The words continue strong, speaking of a "hiding place from the wind, and a covert from the tempest; as rivers of water in a dry place, as the shadow of a great rock in a weary land" (32:2). The people of this community were doing their very best to create such a covert.[34]

How Covert formally got its name, or even when its residents started calling their community by that heavily loaded word, is a story much garbled by time. Some claim William Packard came up with the name, while others say a teacher in the community did. Intriguingly, township records from as early as 1866 show that the post office was calling itself Covert, and the first church founded in Covert, in 1870, was called Covert Congregational Church, even though it would be six years before the township officially had its name changed from Deerfield to Covert. Perhaps it is appropriate that the name of this community — so radical in its commitment to equality and the protection of its integrated nature — should also have a mysterious origin.

Although it may have looked like wilderness to the Yankees, by 1855 layers of culture had already been spread thick across the land. This was no tabula rasa. For centuries many peoples had been interacting and living on the land: Algonquin, Potawatomi, Métis, French, and British all had been laying claim, farming, hunting, warring, and living together. Although the Yankee perception of the native people who had been there before them was of wild and indolent savages who hunted and made war, these were in fact a people who had been farmers for generations, growing corn, beans, and squash and occasionally hunting game in a wilderness that had been so overhunted for so long that deer were rare and hard to come by and bear and beaver had vanished. The indigenous people of the Great Lakes region had been in close contact with Europeans for almost two hundred years and, by the mid 1850s, were familiar with the ways, culture, and minds of people from across the ocean. Indeed, these were a people of the diaspora, many of whom could claim European, African, and Indian nations as kin.[34]

One reason for this melding was the fact that the region around the Great Lakes, including Michigan, had for two centuries been a haven for Native American refugees fleeing from European settlement and violence in the East.[35] These refugees had to beg for the right to settle on a piece of land owned by other indigenous peoples who already, and rightly, claimed it as their own. Here were no romantic notions of "hunting rights" or communal property, but, rather, sophisticated concepts of farming, land use, and ownership easily recognizable to any European. Even the United States government recognized this, since from the time of the Revolution they had been sending their troops to the region to fight against people who fully understood that their property was being stolen from them.[36]

By the 1820s, however, things had begun to change very fast. The treaties to force the Indians from their homelands, the opening of the Erie Canal in 1825, and the forcible and brutal removal by the military of the true owners of the lands in Michigan led to massive land speculations that arose as

Michigan was "opened" to settlement. After a series of treaties, the United States, tired of talking, sent troops to hunt down the Potawatomi and any other peoples for whom Michigan was home. Families were physically forced from their home-steads and farms and made to march until those who survived were dumped on land west of the Mississippi, land that was already home to other people who had rightful claim to it, a fact obvious to the starving and heartsick refugees.[37]

Van Buren County, in which Covert Township resided, was one of the last regions of the lower portion of the state to be opened to settlement. These new residents envisioned them-selves as Yankees, which meant that they were fierce about com-munity institutions, organizing local governments, churches, and schools in their new settlements as quickly as they could.[38] Even when the settlers there were living in rough log cabins, struggling just to survive, they still made it a priority to put to-gether some form of local township government. Although early on there were probably fewer men than open positions, they were able to elect one another to the posts of supervisor, treasurer, clerk, Justice of the Peace and his four deputies, drain commissioner, highway commissioner, up to eight high-way overseers, and six school inspectors.[39]

These men ran the township. But what was a township in the nineteenth century? Townships in Michigan defined re-gions within the counties. Some included villages; others of-fered little more than crossroads intersecting in the middle of woods and farm fields. The residents of these townships, how-ever, felt a strong tie to this imagined plot of land. These were their communities. Covert happened to have a small village in its center, also called Covert (often delineated on census records as the Village of Covert). Apart from the outcroppings of lumbermen's shanty houses around the sawmills, the village was by far the most concentrated group of dwellings in the township, with between thirty and fifty homes and, at various times, a town hall, a general store or two, a church, and even, during the peak of its population and prosperity, a hotel. The rest of the residents were scattered across the township. Settlers could choose to build a home in the middle of their land or right up against the border of their neighbor's property.

Usually, however, neighbors' homes were heard, not seen. Rural life offers an odd intimacy. Neighbors could pass each other by on dirt roads with a nod and a tip of the hat, but then the cows would get loose, a child would fall ill, a fire would start, and all that was private and contained would be revealed. Sometimes it was just the weather — the right kind of still summer night when the thick air would carry noises a far way. Laughter, a fight, an unhappy pig, the rich thunk of a butter churn, singing, even a gunshot as someone tried to keep a possum away from the henhouse.

But this settled life was a long way off for the first white settlers of Covert, who thought of themselves as a people of strict morals and disciplined order who could bring "civilization" to what they perceived as the depths of the wilderness. In some ways they succeeded. Even before Covert was officially formed, men from out East had been platting the land. This was a process in which they mapped the terrain, then laid a perfect grid across the landscape that roads and boundaries would follow with little easement given for the rises of topography and the swerving of streams. Every half mile another grid was laid down on a perfect north-south axis, and each of the roads that followed these grids was numbered, making the land logical. These lines ran so true that to this day residents of the region often do not use terms such as left and right but go by the compass.

After traveling the difficult and winding routes to their settlements, the Yankees must have found relief in the lines that had been laid across the land, even if they existed only on the maps that made their wilderness look civilized. And what a journey it was. For those whites coming to the Midwest during this time, their travels were defined by lodging. After a day of struggling through forests, slogging through bog holes and swamps, and wading through rivers, travelers held the hope that at the end of each long day there would be some form of shelter they could share with its occupants. As darkness fell they would have sniffed the air for the smell of smoke or listened for the faraway bark of a dog, indicators that warmth, light, and, with any luck, food would be found nearby. (Fairy tales with stories of a comforting light glimpsed far off through heavy woods were improbable since glass windows were rare. Light might leak through the badly chinked logs of a cabin, but even candles and lanterns were scarce, and the glow of firelight does not go far.) Once a place was found, the most that weary travelers could expect would be a rough cabin, with possibly an adjoining lean-to. Sleep was a shared experience. A husband and wife oftentimes found themselves sharing floor or even bed space with strangers of both sexes. Travelers could only hope that their hosts were hospitable and honest. Caroline Kirkland, a woman of European descent traveling with her husband to Michigan in the 1830s, wrote to her friends in the East about their adventures starting a new life on the Michigan frontier. Although she tempers her accounts with much humor, mocking her own inexperience with the rough life Michigan offered, it is obvious that traveling through Michigan was brutal and exhausting. At one point along the way, they lodged in a "wretched inn" run by a drunkard who terrorized his wife, family, and any guests that may have had to take shelter under his roof.[40]

Nevertheless, for all these trials, Caroline and her husband were white and could expect whatever hospitality could be offered by the families along the way. How different the experience for pioneers of African descent. In many cases those free black families traveling to the Midwest had a better claim to the label American than those whites whose families had lived for only a generation or two in the new nation. People of African descent had arrived in the eastern United States in the early 1600s, when Shakespeare was still alive and the United States was still known as the New World. Some of these early arrivals were brought over as indentured servants who, like their white counterparts, were expected to work their way to freedom and land ownership. Soon, however, those of African descent arriving on colonial shores were slaves with diminished hopes of ever gaining freedom. During this colonial period racial lines and identities were much more fluid than they would become in the nineteenth century, and many more opportunities existed for blacks to mingle with others.[41] Also during this period some people of African descent were able to buy their own freedom or were freed by their masters. By the time of the Revolutionary War, small pockets of free blacks were living in most of the newly formed states along the East Coast, with particular concentrations in Maryland, Virginia, and Pennsylvania.[42] The Revolutionary War swelled their numbers, for slaves took up arms in the cause of American liberty, and if they survived the many battles they saw, they were sometimes freed.[43]

By the 1830s the color line was being drawn with bolder strokes, and slaveholding Southern whites increasingly found the presence of free blacks in their midst intolerable. (Some were even slave owners like themselves, making a lie the white-supremacist argument that blacks were so far inferior to them that they could not function without white "protection" and direction.[44]) Slave rebellions made things even worse. While there had been smaller uprisings, and would continue to be, the Nat Turner rebellion was by far the best known and most feared by Southern whites. Nat Turner was a literate and eloquent young black man living enslaved in Virginia who believed that God had ordained him to free those in bondage, including himself, by any means necessary. In August of 1831 he acted on this belief. He and his followers started by killing Turner's owners, then turned on other whites in the region, killing sixty within a twenty-four-hour period. The end of their revolt was swift and total. State and federal troops marched into the area and slaughtered at least a hundred slaves, and three free blacks were hanged, although there was little evidence that they had had a role in the rebellion.[45] And the repercussions were terrible. By the mid 1830s North Carolina prohibited any free person of African descent from traveling more than two counties from their home. It was made illegal for free blacks to preach, and most Southern states took away their right to free assembly, which meant that throughout the South no free blacks could gather in large groups, even to worship in a church (although they were given a small loophole in which they were allowed to worship as long as they were led by a white minister).[46] Even before Turner's rebellion, life for a Southern free black was beset with difficulties. If they were judged to be not in "good" employ, they could be forcibly "bonded" out to a white person, and many children were torn from their parents' homes at the age of twelve to be bonded to a stranger until they turned twenty-one.[47] By the eve of the Civil War, most Southern states were seriously considering passage of laws that would enslave all of their free black populations.[48]

In those crucial twenty years between 1830 and 1850, more than 32,500 African Americans walked their way to a new life in the Midwest.[49] Their leaving was, in many ways, the first "Great Migration." By 1850 fully one-eighth of all free African Americans lived in the Midwestern states.[50] Behind each statistic was a tale of extraordinary courage. Free blacks had to travel through slave states, where every step they took could lead them straight into bondage or worse. Some chose to travel the paths, but only at night, and for them the sound of a dog barking in the darkness or the sharp scent of burning did not mean welcome but danger. Most traveled in goodly numbers, for even though they possessed all the correct documentation to prove that they were free, in slave states they could still be seen as walking wealth, ripe for the picking. Slavers were known to overpower small bands and then destroy their free papers and sell them to anyone willing to ignore their pleas. A large enough band, however, could attract attention. One such group, traveling to the Midwest in the 1830s, was indeed stopped by some white men who demanded that they show proof that they were free. This large group made up of a number of black families had already planned for just such a confrontation and refused to stop, having decided that anyone making such a request was already proving themselves hostile. The whites, however, took long stakes and drove them through the wheel spokes, causing the wagons to come to a lurching halt. One of the travelers, Martha Walden, decided to act. She had very light skin, and she hoped that could save them. She stood up and, in a voice she must have tried to make sound as irate as possible, told the men that she was white and in charge of the group. She then told her fellow travelers to remove the pieces of wood stopping their wheels and get moving. The crowd of white men stood back and let them pass.[51]

Once at their destination, however, these brave travelers would still have had to contend with the fact that not one of the Midwestern states or territories warmly welcomed African American settlement. Almost every Midwestern state had "Black Codes," laws that were created by whites dead set against the idea of blacks entering the state, much less settling there. Many of these codes required that before a black person even traveled across a state, he or she had to pay an exorbitant "bond." Additionally, they were required to go before a local judge with written evidence that they were free.[52] If they failed to do so, there could be a terrible price to pay. For a while both Illinois and Iowa required that the labor of those of African descent who were found guilty of breaking their Black Codes could be sold at public auction to the highest bidder.[53] This was little better than the slave block in New Orleans, and it is certain that the white creators of these laws hoped blacks would be intimidated by the similarities. But even after slavery was gone, Midwestern Black Codes laws persisted.[54]

Covert's growth came a little later than this initial wave of black migrants to the Midwest. This meant that some of the first black settlers in Covert were second-generation Midwesterners — second-generation survivors. For them the Midwest was home. Between 1860 and 1870 Covert grew from 200 to 681 residents, and most of the whites were from regions far outside Michigan. It is likely that when the first African Americans arrived there, in 1866, the vast majority of adult residents were from New York. The rest were quite a mix. One of the smallest groups comprised four Southerners, who were outnumbered even by those who had just recently arrived in the country. James Dobbyn came with the first group of Canadians, in 1854, impressing the other new settlers by the fact that his group had no pack animals but carried all their belongings on their own backs.[55] By 1870 almost fifty Canadians lived in the township. Then there were the Europeans who had come straight from the Old World to the

New: almost twenty people from England, a couple from Scotland, and eleven from Germany. A sizable contingent of settlers had been living in other parts of the Midwest, as well as, officially, nine Pokagons (a minority within a minority, Catholic Potawatomi) who, not surprisingly, tried to keep themselves off federal census records as best they could in order to protect themselves from any further removals.[56]

The Pokagons had affiliated themselves with the French Catholics just before the Second Treaty of Chicago, in 1833. The first treaty, of 1821, had forced them to give up their rights to land in southwestern Michigan, and now they were being pressured, along with the Ottawa and Ojibwe, to give up their homelands west of Lake Michigan.[57] This affiliation split the Potawatomi around 1831, when Topinabee, a supporter of Baptist missionaries, broke away from his older adopted brother Pokagon, who had allied himself with the Catholic missionaries.[58] Many who followed Pokagon's lead, who were called Pokagons, had been forced off their land near Notre Dame, Indiana, by the federal government and ended up in a large settlement in Cass County, where they hunted and farmed, teaching the first settlers there how to farm in their unique and productive way.[59]

Pokagon's affiliation proved fruitful, as his group won the right, with the help of the Catholic Fathers, to stay in Michigan while the rest of the Potawatomi were forced to leave. Most of the other Potawatomi peoples of Michigan and Indiana were brutally rounded up in 1838, including Chief Menominee, who had refused to sign the removal treaty.[60]

Those who managed to stay or make it back to Michigan tried everything to survive, even assimilation. Their chances were slim. When Michigan became a territory, in 1805, it had the smallest number of whites of any section of the Northwest Territories, with 4,800, compared with 24,000 in Indiana (in 1800) and 230,000 in Ohio (in 1803). There were, however, many Native Americans; fully 32,000 were counted in the Michigan and Wisconsin territories, although there were almost certainly more who wisely refused to be found by census takers. During the 1830s the white population in Michigan exploded during the period known as Michigan Madness. By 1840 the white population had expanded nearly tenfold, to 36,400. Michigan's Potawatomi population, on the other hand, had dwindled to about 2,500 by 1835.[61]

The Mota, Toquin, and Pokagon families that came to Covert in the 1850s were intent on preserving their language and lifeways.[62] (In an ironic turn of events, they may have ended up buying federal land in Covert in the mid 1850s, probably with the federal compensation money they had been given.)[63]

Because the Pokagons were not considered citizens, voting and holding office were officially denied them. Nevertheless, in 1860, both "Seatons" Mota and Joseph "Tackquin" are listed as voting in April and November. By 1868, Seatons Mota actually ran for and won a post to oversee roadwork in his section of the township. This meant that he could make sure that township and state funds were used to better the land near their settlement.[64] As the township's population grew, however, the Pokagons withdrew, segregating themselves from those who could threaten erosion or extinction of their culture.

Despite the fact that Covert's population was quickly growing in the 1860s, in reality it was still very much a skeletal frontier community, and life was extremely difficult for all the settlers there. This was a world of scarcity, where something as simple as a floor could seem like a luxury.

Effie and Lillian Tripp, two sisters, had come to Covert with their family just before the Civil War. They and their eight other siblings were left alone with their mother when their father had gone off to join the Union army. With ten children to look after, their mother fought her battle of survival on the frontier, trying to preserve life and dignity as best she could. She would walk twelve miles barefoot to the nearest store in order to preserve her shoes; mindful of her appearance, she would put on her shoes just before she entered the town and take them off again for the walk home.[65]

Home, once she reached it, was dim and drafty. The walls that sheltered her and her children looked solid enough but seemed to let most everything in. Theirs was a trough roof, common enough in the area, as it was easy to erect. First the logs had to be split down the middle, then they were hollowed or "troughed" out so that they could be laid in a special pattern, trough side up, with another row laid on top of them, trough side down, where they met. Unfortunately, in the winter the troughs would fill with snow and ice, causing icicles to form on the ceiling and along the walls, often reaching all the way to the floor. The Tripps slept on beds lined with pine boughs, and Effie remembered that her portion of the bed was against the wall, so she had to sleep next to frozen limbs of ice all winter long.

Illness was a constant threat, and there was little the settlers could do to fend it off. Elmira Sinkler, who had come as child from New York to Covert, remembered the winter when she and all five of her brothers and sisters came down with whooping cough. The only remedy her parents could offer was a tonic called maple-wort tea. She described how "father used to go out to the woods and get the moss off from the soft maple limbs and mother would steep it for us children to drink. This was all the medicine we had."[66] Needless to say, death was a common visitor to these early settlers' homes.

These damp shelters were made doubly miserable by the dark. This far north, the sun set early in winter, and the only source of light inside many homes came from firelight or homemade lanterns made of saucers filled with grease from recently slaughtered animals. The grease seemed to create more eye-singeing smoke than light. Holes in cabins were rare, and any openings that were not meant as chimneys were most often covered with roughly cured hides. These early settlers all shared a uniform memory that lasted through their old age — the day when the first lantern was brought to the cabin, or a mother had tallow fine enough to make candles, and finally, pure light shone in their darkness.[67] Not surprisingly, the frontier is most often known by historians as a place of intolerance and violence, where survival depended on scrabbling for limited resources.[68]

By the time the first people of African descent arrived in Covert, the township was only ten years old, but much had happened. The turmoil that had started in the Midwest had given way to open war. No longer did blacks traveling through the Midwest have to fear slave raiders, but the fear of capture had been supplanted by the dread that true freedom was nowhere to be found.

Chapter 2

The Journey: 1860–1866

"The truth is, the nigger is an unpopular institution in the free states. Even those who are unwilling to rob them of all the rights of humanity, and are willing to let them have a spot on earth on which to live and to labor and to enjoy the fruits of their toil, do not care to be brought into close contact with them."

— Editorial from the *Illinois State Journal*,
March 22, 1862[1]

She must have been so tired of walking. Elizabeth Conner was moving, and moving in the Midwest in 1866 meant walking, walking for days through wilderness, through strangers. The wilderness pressed so close that even horses had trouble passing through the roots that tripped and branches that scratched.

Elizabeth almost certainly walked with a group of roughly twenty, although only ten of them were adults.[2] Old experiences, old wounds, had taught these travelers that there was strength in numbers and in arms. Elizabeth's husband and her brothers-in-law all had weapons she knew had killed many a

Southern white man not long ago. So she walked with dear Nancy and Abigail, and they walked alongside husbands. Strangers stared at those dark warriors, and their wives must have had the same urge. The men had walked together for years over hundreds of miles, walked through mud above their knees, walked through the wrecked bodies of their dead comrades, walked straight into gunfire when everything in them was telling them to run away. Now they walked together, with their unfamiliar children, their long-imagined wives now real, into a dreamed future they planned to make true, a future of fairness and prosperity.

Like many pioneers in America's past, they had left a stable and sure place to find a more successful life. That place was the only home Elizabeth had ever known, Mount Pleasant, Cass County, Michigan. Cass County had given shelter to a group of Quakers in the 1830s who then made it home to any blacks who wanted to come — and they came by the hundreds.[3] Some were escaping slaves, rebelling against the idea that they were owned by anyone. Others were long free but sought the freedoms the South would no longer offer them. In Cass County they were able to attend schools, farm their own land, and raise their families.

This was more than unusual; it was feared. In the antebellum Midwest, although some white settlers were willing to use African American slave labor, most were averse to the idea of African Americans living near them, especially if they were free; this attitude extended deep into the new northern territories. As a legislative committee in Ohio made clear in 1832, free blacks were considered more of a threat than slaves, for they were seen as a "corrupting influence," and more important, they infringed upon white employment opportunities.[4]

Elizabeth's father, Henry Shepard, had been among the hundreds who sought shelter in Cass County before the war and who had managed to escape census takers and slave catchers to make a home south of Canada, a home in a nation that was rightly his.

Until he turned twenty-one, Henry Shepard had been owned by someone. Henry promised himself that on his twenty-first birthday he would liberate himself, and he did, walking north as best as he could. But north was the direction the winter came from, howling in hard, and the most freedom he found was a swamp where he could hide. Henry's feet slowly froze and rotted from the wet ground, but that pain was not as terrible as the loss of liberty, and he must have gone down running, still trying to move even after the dogs found him and white men recaptured him.

The man who thought of himself as Henry's owner may have taken one look at Henry's destroyed feet and felt sure that here was a safe slave, one who would literally never run again. But as soon as he deemed himself recovered, Henry made another bid for freedom. This time he was successful and kept walking north on those rotten feet until he had walked all the way to Canada.[5]

Maybe Canada ended up being too cold for a man who had been brought low by a winter. Michigan wasn't easy, but it was easier, and more settled. And it gave Henry a place to become a hero. Although he managed to keep the fact secret from most who knew him, for many years he was a conductor on the

Underground Railroad, bringing escaping slaves from Cass County to the next station in Schoolcraft, and sometimes beyond. He must have been determined that others would not suffer, as he had, to find the way to freedom.[6] He married, had a family, had Elizabeth. And then the war came. What could possess an old man, a man with family and a home, a man with freedom, to walk back into the land that had enslaved him? All that had happened to him in those first twenty-one years of his life must have risen up in him, must have taken him to that enlistment station. And then Henry walked again, walked all the way back to the South with a gun in his hand, and almost all the black men of Cass County went with him.

Some have argued that Midwestern racism was worse than the racism of the South. As an editor of an Iowa paper wrote in 1862, "It has long been manifest that there was a far greater prejudice existing against association with the negro at the North than at the South."[7] Obviously, this is an old argument. Yet the Midwest was also a beacon of hope for both blacks and whites intent on settling and creating a new way of being together. These sentiments may not have been popular, but they were strong enough to create open warfare before the Civil War and strong enough to put through some of the earliest civil rights laws passed in this country. Henry Shepard did not walk on injured feet to settle in Michigan because it was worse than being enslaved. He probably would have agreed with the historian and sociologist Charles Payne, who wrote, "The Southern racial system, in fact, allowed for a great deal of personal contact across racial lines, perhaps more so than in other parts of the country; it just had to be contact on terms defined by white people."[8]

Now it was Henry's daughter's turn to find a new and better life with her four children, Johnny, Irene, Mary, and little Lillie, her sweet flower, her new baby. Johnny and Irene were born before the war and would still have been warming to their father, whose face had been but a photograph for more than two long years. But Mary and Lillie were homecoming babies — Mary just toddling at two, Lillie still in her mother's arms — new children in a new world.

Elizabeth and the women who walked with her — Nancy and Abigail — had all watched their men leave for war. They knew why their men had to go, they knew all the million reasons why, some told as tales on a winter evening, others as secret and hurting as nightmares. Still, it had been so hard to see them walk away, their babies weeping, the whole world weeping, and cheering too.

Nancy had been luckier than many, having only one baby to care for while Joseph was gone to war. There are no surviving descriptions of Nancy, but there are many of her beloved and adventurous husband. His friends described him as "a true raw-boned man," "a gritty man," who worked "often when he was not able." When Nancy's true raw-boned man enlisted, all the army wrote was "eyes and hair, black; complexion, brown; height, 5'10"."[9] But he was much more than that to Nancy.

Nancy's brother, William Frank Conner, had left Elizabeth with two children under the age of four. But those may as well have been Nancy's own, for she and Elizabeth had shared a home for the long and lonely time their men were gone.[10] It was Elizabeth who had been at her side during little Joseph's birth; it had been Elizabeth who was able to read aloud William's letters home, giving them both comfort. And when the men came home, both Elizabeth and Nancy bore children of the homecoming within months of each other, Elizabeth's Lillie and Nancy's Franklin. When, a few years later, Nancy finally had a little girl, she named her Lilly, after her niece, her beloved friend's daughter.[11]

Now here they were, the summer of 1866, less than a year after the men's return, going to the land William and his friend and brother-in-law Himebrick Tyler had bought in Covert. They would have certainly told her of it, lovely land, all good timber and rich soil, and few people there.

Cass County had long been cleared for farming, but as the travelers walked farther into Van Buren County, they walked deeper into woods. These were trees that they would soon know as well as family. There were the locusts: tough, covered in thorns, and repellent to insects. Locusts ignored spring, standing with branches bare, defying warm days, nesting birds, and the full green leaves on the branches of all the other trees. Finally, begrudgingly, they would fill out with small leaves, miserly of their green. But every second or third year, not regular enough to be counted on so always a surprise, the locusts would bloom, and for a brief time the North Woods turned into a scene from far Arabia. Long heavy clumps of jasmine-scented blossoms would droop from every surface of the tree, even the trunk, gracefully hiding the long barbs that could draw blood from unsuspecting fingers, a veritable rose of a tree. This flowering would come so late in the spring that one could whisper that they really were a summer flower — they even smelled best when the air was warmest — but deep in the heart one knew that this was spring for the locust trees, well and truly, and they were blooming, like some children do, in their own sweet time.

But it was not spring, nor summer, that brought color to Covert; it was the fall. And the color could come overnight. First to change were the weed trees, the sumac and the sassafras, which sent suckers out under the loam to create clumps and stands of themselves in patches where there was sun. The sassafras would turn a pale yellow, but the sumac would bloom into deep and startling red, shedding its leaves to reveal dark velvet cones of seeds that looked right pretty in the winter when wearing a cap of snow. From the scrubby weed trees to their tall companions — the cherry and oak, maple and locust — it was as if the color were a fire and the whole forest were burning.

It had been good timber that had almost kept Nancy's parents from leaving the South, that and the familiarity of friends and kin; but her parents, William Bright Conner and Elizabeth Schrugs Conner, had dreamed of raising their family free of the racism they had known all their lives. They were free blacks, needing no "benevolent" masters to blossom, strong and beautiful, and they were more than able to compete with whites for business and success. There was no mistaking the African origins of the Conners and the Tylers. The intensity and the richness of their skin gave lie to the fact that lighter was better, more pleasing, more able to succeed in the world.[12]

The Conner and Tyler families had come from Snow Hill, North Carolina. Their roots were in the Carolinas, almost two centuries deep by the time they decided to leave.[13] Snow Hill was the seat of Greene County, a small county in the middle of the eastern half of the state, and was named for the white sand that lay under the forests and shone through the bare patches at the tops of the hills, near enough to snow for the South.

Nancy had walked north with her brother, William Frank Conner, as well as many other Conner kin and the Tyler brothers. She must have told William's wife, Elizabeth Shepard, of that journey, of moments of beauty so strong that even terror and tiredness could not bar its acknowledgment, of standing on top of a high pass in the Blue Ridge Mountains seeing the rain fall in a valley far below where they stood. Nancy, only a child at the time, was filled with wonder that her small self could be higher than the clouds that lay spread at her feet.[14] Unlikely as it may have seemed to them then, home, at the end of it all, would be a place of gently rolling wooded hills, with sand peeping through at the top and real snow to cover them all.

Though they were free, the large party that traveled north before the war was often stopped on their journey through the slave states, but their "free papers," legal documents that attested to their status, were honored. Despite the group's good team of horses and a wagon in which the youngest children could ride, progress was slow. Far into their journey, but still in the slave states, an aunt lost her free papers. The next time they were stopped by a group of white "patrollers," they were helpless to save her, and she was taken. The effect this must have had on the children and their families can only be imagined. Terrified and grieving, the group decided it would thereafter travel only at night until reaching the free states.

They were not out of danger yet, even when they finally reached the shores of the Ohio River. On the morning they were planning to cross to a new freedom, three white men stopped by their camp and tried to persuade William Bright Conner to trade his horses. He was unwilling to do so, and the traders soon left. Before long, though, one of the men came riding back and told Conner to pack up his belongings and gather his group as quickly and quietly as possible because his companions intended to ambush them at the bank of the river and sell them into slavery. The man told them he would return at dusk, dressed in black, to lead them away from any pursuers and guide them to another crossing, just downstream. The Conners then had to make a terrible decision. They had firsthand experience of the treachery and cruelty of whites who saw them only as chattel. They could cross the river at the point they were sure of and soon be on freedom's shore, or they could risk trusting a white man who seemed willing to betray his friends for their sake. In an agony of uncertainty, the Conners finally decided to wait for the man to return. While packing up their belongings, they must have tried to calm the children, putting on a brave face for the youngest of the group, but everyone must have been on edge.

The man finally returned, alone, as he had promised. He

motioned to them that they were not to speak to him or to one another during their flight. All night the group made their torturous and silent way through the woods until it was almost dawn. The adults must have been so turned around they could not have escaped an ambush, even if they had wanted to. But then they saw the river through the trees. Their rescuer directed them to a crossing where they were able to pass unmolested. As they did so, they could see the other crossing and were able to hear an angry roar from the mob that was waiting there for them.

They had reached the free states.

The Conners saw themselves as people with the freedom to choose, and they were willing to pick up and keep walking to find a better life, a choice they made over and over again, going from Indiana to Canada to Michigan. It was Michigan that would become home.[15]

And then the war came. During those difficult days of decision, William Frank Conner must have thought of his aunt, somewhere in the South, enslaved. As a child he had been powerless to help her when the slave raiders stole her away. Now, however, he was a man, and he could fight, fight for her freedom, fight for the freedom of all his race.

The walk had worked.

William Frank Conner probably had no way of knowing it, but back in Snow Hill, North Carolina, another William Conner, a member of the clan who had stayed behind, was forcibly conscripted into Greene County's Third Regiment to clean Confederate soldiers' clothes. His same-named relative in Michigan took up a gun to shed blood, possibly on those very uniforms.[16]

Like William and his kin, many black men from Cass County volunteered. These brave men knew better than most of their white counterparts the land they were going to and the kind of men they would be fighting. And yet, they had to struggle for the right to become soldiers. Many whites in the Midwest were terrified of the idea of dark men with guns killing white men. The editor of a Midwestern newspaper was horrified that black men would be considered for the service, writing, "The idea of calling on *him* . . . to fight our battles . . . is not only a confession of our own weakness and cowardice . . . it is the last outcropping of a local insanity."[17] Others had such a low opinion of "Negroes" that they thought no black man would have the courage to fight. But the men in Elizabeth's life prevailed, as did many other fathers, husbands, friends, and brothers who left the women to face life without them. What none of them could have known as they watched their men march away was that the rate of mortality among black troops would be 40 percent higher than for white Union troops, due in part to the Confederates' "no quarter" policy against any black soldiers captured, meaning that a black Union soldier going into battle could be pretty certain that he would either win or die.[18]

When their men left in 1863, Elizabeth invited Nancy, her sister-in-law, to stay with her at Pleasant Hill. Nancy had been married to her husband, Joseph, for only nine months before he left with all the others. Barely twenty, she was expecting her first child; Elizabeth had little John and Irene. There were many women around to help with birthing, to aid in raising the children, to tend the fields, to milk the cows, to butcher the hogs, to dig the graves, to do everything needed. They worked hard, the women, the old men, and the children, and the results were extraordinary: production quotas for their county did not falter during the war; they flourished. More came from the women's work than had ever been produced by men in the past.[19] Maybe the hard work kept the fear at bay.

William sent letter after letter to Elizabeth as his regiment moved across the South, letters she kept with her after the war was over, on her walk through the Michigan wilderness toward Covert. He tried to reassure her, telling her of all the familiar friends he had around him — after all, as he reminded her, "we have got nearly all the men there in Cass County in this Regt." He was recognized and commended, and he changed ranks upward so quickly that Elizabeth must have had a hard time keeping track, until she finally grasped that she was married to a sergeant, a man who had power over many in his company.[20]

In eloquent letters he sent information she could share with the women, of their husbands, fathers, sons, and brothers. There were stories to make her laugh and there was love to make her weep. He sent her almost every penny he made, to make her life possible and to pay off the land he and Hime-brick Tyler had bought in Covert just before they left. In defense of the fact that he kept a bit of money for his own use, he lightly wrote, "You know I am a great hand for my belly," adding, "I have to spend a great deal for what ever I want for

I don't know how long I will live and I don't mean to be in debt to my Belly."

Elizabeth's husband had always been a businessman, and he continued, even on the front. Indeed, it must have made her nervous, the amounts he sent back to her. How could he be doing well, in a place that in her heart held only danger and horror? When she questioned him, he wrote, on November 19, 1864, "Dear wife . . . I want to prepare a good living for you and the children if I never see you again . . . [A]lso you want to know if I got this money honest that I have been making. I will leave it to your option. If trade such as buying and selling and making close trade and keeping a sharp lookout is honest then I make an honest living. . . . If I were lost from this army I could make a thousand dollars a year."

But soon all business would be forgotten. Just days after writing the letter, William, Himebrick, Joseph, and "nearly all the men of Cass Ct" would march into "the very mouth of death."[21]

Elizabeth treasured that letter of November 19 for years afterward, holding as it did her husband's promises and dreams for their future, his sweet words that she may well have thought would be the last she would ever read from him. It is more than likely that news of the Battle of Honey Hill, South Carolina, made its way to Pleasant Hill, Michigan, as newspapers were quick to catch the story of the tragic heroism of the Michigan men facing battle for the first time.

The Battle of Honey Hill took place on November 30, 1864, in support of General William T. Sherman's march to the sea. This was a battle fought primarily by black men against white, with at least six United States Colored Troops (USCT) involved, including the Massachusetts Fifty-fourth and Fifty-fifth, as well as the Thirty-fifth USCT, commanded by Harriet Beecher Stowe's brother, Colonel James Beecher. The Confederate-controlled crest of Honey Hill was covered with man-made defenses that a captain of the Massachusetts Fifty-fifth Colored Regiment described as

> a substantial open earthwork, pierced by four guns, extended two hundred feet on either side of the road, on the crest of an abrupt slope of about twenty feet. The ground immediately in front of the entrenchments was comparatively open, but at the distance of about one hundred and fifty yards a shallow and sluggish stream, expanding into a swamp with a heavy growth of trees and dense underbrush, ran along the whole Confederate front.[22]

The soldiers from Michigan almost certainly knew that they were marching against a foe who could well be intent upon their slaughter even if they surrendered and were taken prisoner. Seven months earlier, in April of 1864, Confederate troops had captured a federal fort in Tennessee called Fort Pillow. Almost half of the troops stationed there were black. The American troops, both white and black, put up a good fight but lost the battle and surrendered to the secessionist soldiers. The Confederate troops then proceeded to slaughter the soldiers, while their leader, General Nathan Bedford Forrest, stood by and watched. Tents sheltering wounded soldiers were set on fire, and hundreds of black soldiers were murdered.[23]

The first charge, led by the Massachusetts Fifty-fifth, was mowed down by the "murderous fire" of "grape, canister and bullets at short range."[24] The commanders of the United States forces faced a dreadful problem. Some of their most powerful cannons were now close to the enemy line, but many of the men sent to fire them and many of the horses needed to haul back the artillery had been slaughtered. As night fell the commanders decided to send in William and the men of the 102nd USCT to retrieve the artillery. Some of the Michigan men were assigned to protect their comrades with covering fire, and as they began firing, the rest marched in a steady line toward their deadly goal — the retrieval of the cannonry and any men still left alive around them. The covering fire gave little protection against the "fearful" Confederate musketry of Honey Hill, and "many were wounded quite severely . . . [and] kept on fighting, while the blood was flowing from their wounds."[25] But they did not give up. There in the darkness filled with the terrible noise of guns and pain, the Michigan men succeeded in what many must have thought was an impossible mission. Their maneuvers resulted in the death of twenty-three Michigan men, the first battle fatalities experienced by the regiment.[26] When added to all the Union dead and wounded, the totals were 91 killed, 631 wounded, 26 missing.[27]

Did William ever talk to Elizabeth of such horrors? In many ways the men walking through the Michigan woods two years after that battle, walking with their families to a new home, shared a bond that the women could never be a part of, a bond of blood memories. As members of the 102nd, William,

Himebrick, John, and Joseph would have witnessed awful carnage that day, carnage that horrified even the Confederate soldiers, who saw before them black soldiers whose bodies "lay five deep . . . horribly mutilated by shells."[28] William and his comrades had to run through and over that sad and terrible mass, risking their own lives to save the few who survived. A high-ranking white officer who witnessed their actions wrote his report of that battle, his astonishment evident:

> Now such bravery I have never seen before. . . . After having been three and a half years in the field and participated in sixteen different engagements, I never saw men exhibit such bravery in battle . . . some were shot through and through the fleshy part of the arm who have not gone to the hospital, but after having their wounds dressed have come to their company quarters, and scarcely seemed to notice their wounds. If such a thing had occurred in the [white] regiment I formerly belonged to, such a wound would have been good for a three-month's stay in some hospital at Philadelphia or Baltimore.[29]

Despite such extraordinary actions, the battle was lost to the Confederates. But the Battle of Honey Hill convinced white military leaders that the soldiers of the 102nd USCT were worthy not only of respect but of praise. In the beginning, when the troop was organized, even "those [whites] connected with it were subjects of derision." But the battle changed everything. A commander of the 102nd wrote, "The white regiment which fought next to ours held our men in highest estimation, and expressed their preference to fight beside our regiment rather than any other regiment in the department."[30]

Of course, death did not find the men only on the battle-field but also on dank ground and in bloodstained hospital tents. Nancy and Elizabeth must have grieved with their friend Louisa Matthews, who was, like them, at home with her babies, and now her husband was gone forever, dead in some hostile hospital in South Carolina. Worse yet, the war was already over when he died, brought down by disease far away, before he could get home to his family.[31]

Besides shared concerns and losses, the women also had their own unique bonds, bonds that could never be shared by the men. They had held each others' hands while they labored to give birth. They, too, witnessed death. To be a woman in nineteenth-century America was to be always at risk. The very giving of life could take it. Just as the men were fighting to bring about a new world, the women were sacrificing their lives to bring about the next generation, the generation they hoped would enjoy a free America.

Of all the losses this band of survivors was grieving, the loss of Zylphia Tyler, Himebrick's wife, may have been the sorest. There are no records of what caused her death, but she would not have been alone as she passed, for the other women stood by her bed. Those women, the ones who were young and strong of arm and back, would have dug her grave and laid her body down as her children grieved. And, finally, they would have raised their voices in song, even as their singing tongues tasted the bitter salt of sorrow.[32]

Himebrick must have been adrift without her. In the war he

had seen so many taken by death, had helped to bury so many in the gray sorrow of clay, but he had not been able to bury his own wife. He himself had barely been able to escape that time of war with his life. Leaving Beaufort Island, where he was stationed off the coast of South Carolina, he had been sent to get whiskey for the company. But something happened: their little boat was wrecked, swamped, tipped over, and he had to watch his companions drown. On that dreadful Carolina day, he was the one left alive, clinging to what little remained in life, hoping to stay afloat. For hours he gripped the edge of the boat and years later would blame the deep pain in his bones on that experience.[33] All he had now were the memories of strangers' deaths and of five years of sweet marriage. His children were solid enough, his little strangers, Cornelius, James, and Octavius, who walked with him on the way to the new home and the new life their father had promised them in Covert. But Zylphia's death had made Himebrick an oddity in Cass County, a single parent among the two-parent homes that were common in the black community there. Yes, sometimes death took a spouse — Himebrick was not alone in his grieving — but Cass County's African American families were fierce in their commitment to kinship, and the farmhouses were filled with children being raised by both parents.[34]

All of his family must have worried for him. Himebrick was a kind and tender man, particularly fond of children. Elizabeth knew this, for while at war he sent little presents to her son, one time a bright shiny button, promising his nephew candy in exchange for the little trinket when he got back.[35]

Now here was Himebrick planning on walking away from Cass County, walking away from the past, walking to nowhere: the frontier, the wilderness, a place of strangers. Certainly no place where he could find a companion, someone to ease his sorrow and love his children as much as he did.

Was it his brother-in-law Joseph who first mentioned Louisa Matthews? Joseph had known her for years, having attended school in Cass County with her as a young child.[36] Now Louisa was a grown woman, and herself grieving. Like Himebrick, she had lost her spouse, and just when there'd been hope he would return whole. She, too, had the burden of raising children alone. Before Louisa and Himebrick could be together, however, Himebrick had to make a home place for himself and his children in Covert.

The land William and Himebrick had purchased was inland from Lake Michigan. Water was the main means of transport before the Civil War. The dunes cut Covert off completely from the lake, and there were no large rivers to act as roads for new settlers. Most of the land was still in federal hands and going cheap. It was economics that finally drove settlement, not the land itself. Land lining the water was not useful except for a view, and that would not be considered of much value until two generations had passed. There the dunes were high and deeply folded, the sand under the light loam able to grow only a sparse forest. These great sand hills, monstrous giants sleeping along Covert's western side, had hindered settlement, and the trees that succeeded in clinging against the hard wind were huge and often scarred. The largest were strong enough to hold the carcasses of other trees in their limbs, trees that the wind or disease or just sheer lack of light in the undercanopy had tried to fell but that had been caught by their larger neighbors.

These wooded dunes could march three or four deep to the lake and then die at the final defense of the land against the water. These last hills were sometimes the highest, their sandy sides rubbed raw of cover by the almost constant wind and the ever constant erosion of their foundations by the waves. Over the years there would be parries and retreats. Sometimes the land won battles, but the water's war was always won. One year the dunes were safe, the beaches wide and warm, and one could walk for miles along them to neighboring towns or until the width of a river mouth forced retreat. Then there were the years when the water rushed in and tore at the roots of the hills, creating sharp cliffs of sand that would constantly crumble, causing the trees hundreds of feet above to slowly lose their footing and slide down into the inland sea.

But if there was no stability on the coast, farther inland there certainly was in the trees, a vastness of them. The Conners knew the value of trees; William Bright Conner, William Frank Conner's father, had made his fortune off the pines of North Carolina before leaving for the North. This knowledge would prove valuable in Michigan. William Frank Conner chose the best timbered land he could find even though he had no mill nor any use for the trees other than to build his home and barns.[37] While farther south, in Cass County, the land had long been cleared, in Covert the forests were filled with opportunity, for there were pines, oak, and even the lowly locust.

Like these trees Elizabeth was a native of Michigan — and just as stubborn, strong, and deep-rooted. Yet, despite her courage, despite her hope, Elizabeth may well have prayed for herself, and all she loved, that this be the last time they had to walk on unknown land. A possible prayer, a probable plea — let this new land, this place that would be known as Covert, let this be home. Let there be no more walking.

Chapter 3

Rights: 1866–1869

"Came into a new country and worked much together."

— Himebrick Tyler,
Covert, Michigan[1]

Elizabeth and William Conner came with family, a ready-made community. But they were pioneers in the truest sense of the word, pushing past the boundaries of the expected to gain all that they felt was their right. They were not in Covert merely to survive; they were in Covert to thrive.

The first radical move they would make was their arrival. After all, this was the Midwest. Today, the Midwest may conjure visions of a quiet and complacent place, but such was not the case at this time. This was the frontier, a rugged promised land, where many felt a new way of being for the nation could be formed afresh.[2] The Conners and their company were far from alone in their idealism, but their ideals were not always shared in the Midwest. For many whites Elizabeth's presence in this land, and the presence of any like her, was a matter of much contention.

Elizabeth knew this deep in her bones. Ohio, Indiana, Illinois, Wisconsin, Iowa, Nebraska, Kansas, Missouri, and of course Michigan had been, and would continue to be, battlegrounds over black freedom and civil rights. Here in the Midwest, thousands of miles from the cotton fields of Mississippi, was Kansas, where whites had slaughtered one another in the name of preserving or destroying slavery. Here in the Midwest, Nebraska and Missouri legally kept blacks enslaved even after the Civil War was over. Here in the Midwest, people of African descent were subjected to rampant racism even if their blackness was evident only as a ghost in their blood. This meant that a blue-eyed, blond-haired man with skin so pale the blue veins showed through might still be denied the rights of citizenship if someone could prove one of his grandparents looked African. There would have been no investigations needed for Elizabeth's group from Cass County. Joseph Seaton, Nancy's husband, was the lightest among them, but even he was obviously African in descent.[3]

It is difficult to know just how many white Midwesterners hated and feared the very concept of black settlement, even though the number of blacks in each state was relatively small. Even in the earliest frontier days, long before the abolition of slavery, the fear ran strong. A lawyer in Iowa wrote a petition to the state legislature in 1841 opposing abolitionists struggling to overturn the state's racist Black Codes. He warned the politicians that if the codes were tampered with, Iowa would "Change this Spring time of Our Territory to the *Yellowness* of Autumn and the *Blackness and darkness* of Winter would forever blight the *Fair* prospects of our youthful Country and shroud it in a veil of *Brown*." He was careful to place special stress on the words that still bear his emphasis.[4]

Michigan's own Black Codes meant that African Americans seeking to settle were required to post a five hundred dollar bond and possess papers of freedom as early as 1827.[5] This bond was deliberately a prohibitive amount of money at a time when a day laborer could expect to make less than a dollar a day.[6] When the Civil War came, the Illinois Senate, just across Lake Michigan from where Elizabeth Conner and her kin were traveling, added an extra deterrent, a proposition that any black person illegally entering the state would be subject to punishment of a brutal flogging.[7] In both Illinois and Indiana, lesser legal restrictions to African American immigration were operative as late as the 1880s.[8]

But where legislatures ruled, people did not always follow. Indiana may have had some of the harshest Black Codes, but it was also home to many abolitionist settlements and had the second-largest black population in the Midwest. In a few communities across the Midwest, blacks were able to have lives of relative success and freedom. And for all the viciousness of racist Midwesterners, the Republican Party — Lincoln's party and the party of emancipation — was first and foremost a Midwestern party. Formed in Michigan, its first president was from Kentucky and Illinois. While there has been much written on emancipation, the Republicans, and the Civil War, one thing is clear about the followers of this party — in the local newspapers of the Midwest before the war, anyone who stood up publicly for the rights of blacks was a Republican, rarely a Democrat. Republicans may not have been united in their attitudes on slavery or civil rights, but those who were passionately for those causes allied themselves with the Republicans.[9] And it would be a Republican president who would lead the nation as it tried to tear itself apart over slavery.

Just because white Republican men in Covert had fought for the United States, it was no guarantee that they would feel warmly toward the blacks who chose to settle in their community. Indeed, in 1862 Union soldiers from Indiana kept a group of African Americans from crossing the Ohio River into Indiana and freedom by aiming guns at the fugitives. They made it clear through their actions and their shouted epithets that their regiment was not fighting to make their state a haven for blacks.[10] This could easily have been the welcome received by Elizabeth Conner and her family, resulting in black and white Union veterans facing each other in fear and anger.

Instead, there was the surprise of welcome.

The welcome was doubly surprising because the Conners and their group were not the only people of African descent arriving in Covert. There were also the Pompeys.

Indiana natives Washington and Napoleon Pompey were young and single. These brothers were the advance scouts, the adventurers. Their names were noble and grand, their parents' pride in their babies shouted clear and loud. While they were lighter than the Conners and Tylers, racism had not dealt lightly with these young men with dark curling hair and gray eyes or with their family.[11]

Their father, Dawson, and his brother Fielding do not show up in federal census records until 1850, and by then they were fully grown men with families. Their descendants today hold many histories of Dawson and Fielding. All agree that the two were both sons of the same slave woman. Some say that she was so beloved by her master that when she bore Dawson her master's wife became jealous and he had to give the enslaved woman to his brother, who also became enamored of her, and soon she became pregnant with Fielding. Others say that it was just one master who loved his mistress so much that he freed her and her sons to live in Ohio, where the two boys became skilled horsemen, training and riding racehorses.[12] The most secret (at the time) of all the versions is connected to those horses. In this version, told by one of Washington Pompey's granddaughters, either Dawson or Fielding was entrusted by a master with transporting gold and racehorses to a race in a nonslave state. Once in the free state, the daring Pompey took the money and the horses and ran. [13]

If indeed Dawson and Fielding had escaped slavery in order to live free and successful lives in the Midwest, they had every reason to want to guard the details of their past in order to protect their present and their future. This was not at all unusual among people who had made the dangerous choice of freedom. Elizabeth Conner's father did not allow his story of escape to become public until after his death, even though he lived for decades after slavery was abolished.[14]

As for Dawson's sons, Washington and Napoleon, the miracle was their survival. Although they could have passed for white, they wore Africa into battle, joining the Eighth Corp d'Afrique, a Philadelphia-based black regiment, a band of soldiers that would see its men slaughtered at a horrific rate.[15] The brothers fought side by side, protecting each other through the long months of terror and death.

When they tried to return home, they were reminded that it was not only the Confederates that hated them. Black soldiers who had lived for years in Indiana before going off to fight were now prohibited from returning home to their families because they had not followed, to the letter of the law, Indiana's harsh and ever-changing Black Codes. Even if they had shed their blood for their country, they had not paid their Black Code bond to Indiana, and Indiana would not let them in.[16]

Washington and Napoleon had grown up in a state that denied its black residents so much, and they were not going to be denied any more. They went almost straight from Brownsville, Texas, where they had been discharged, to Michigan.[17] They arrived in 1866, at the same time as the Conners, the Tylers, and the Seatons.

Meanwhile, the Conners and their group from Cass County all settled on the land that William and Himebrick had bought at the northeast edge of Covert township. Almost immediately William's father, William Bright Conner, bought forty acres adjoining his son's land, and it is obvious he picked the land for a very specific reason — there was a school on it.[18]

A hint at his motivation can be seen in the actions of the African American John Watson in Illinois. In 1875 Watson leased land that had a local public school on it that, at the time, was teaching only white students. With lease in hand he went to the school board asking for the keys to the school, with the intent of opening its doors to all the children who lived in the region. The school board refused. The black man warned he'd use force, but the head of the school board pulled out a shotgun and threatened to shoot the integrationist. Watson promptly sought a warrant against the man. The case dragged on for a number of years and ultimately came to an unsatisfactory conclusion for Watson.[19]

Integrated education was not just frowned upon by the state of Michigan in 1866, it was illegal and had been for more than twenty-five years.[20] So when William's father, William Bright Conner, bought that land with the school on it, he was not just challenging the local community. While Covert may have been on the frontier, its schools were already a part of the state bureaucracy. There was a school board, whose superintendent sent detailed yearly reports to the state capital.

Covert took the education of its children so seriously that it had hired teachers before preachers and built schools before it even had a meeting hall for local elections.[21] These were not redbrick structures; most were not even white clapboard. They were rough shelters, doubling in some cases as barns. Despite the rough conditions the Covert school board still managed to get its reports to Lansing. Often chatty in tone, they described the condition of the buildings, the health of the students, and even the behavior of the students. As one superintendent wrote in 1864, "The schools have good order morals and behavior good for the backwoods and a new township."[22] And now a group of rabble-rousing blacks had settled in the township, on land that had one of the township's precious schools on it.

Integrated education was a highly contested issue in the nineteenth-century Midwest: most whites across the region were violently opposed to such racial mixing. Indeed, many Midwestern whites were opposed to blacks getting an education in any form. One teacher, Sarah Curtis — who was not even attempting to teach in an integrated school, just to lead a class of all African American children in Gallatin County, Illinois, just after the Civil War — wrote that after months of being ostracized by local whites for her position, she gave up in "utter disgust" at her neighbors' actions.[23]

Covert was a township of the young, with more than half of the 350 settlers there under the age of twenty.[24] There was an overabundance of children, many of whom had probably never seen someone of African descent. So this was not just about education; this was about intimacy. Covert's schools each consisted of one room, with one teacher who oversaw the education of all the children in that school district. The system required that children of different ages and skills teach each other, sitting side by side on benches, leaning over each other's slates to work on sums, holding a book between them as they read aloud. An integrated school meant that a black child who was an excellent reader could well be placed with older white students to help them labor through their McGuffey Reader.[25] The white families of Covert knew all this, and the school board knew that allowing the Conner, Tyler, and Seaton children to attend the local school on William Bright Conner's land would be breaking the law.

Adolphus Sherburn, a member of the school superintendent's board, was only in his early twenties and had come from Canada with his extended family. He and his family had been farming in the area for a few years by 1866. He was uncle to school-age children and, as a single man, had the time to be involved in local politics. The group from Cass County had settled in the school district he oversaw, so it made sense that he go to their home to speak with them. He brought with him a sturdy piece of paper issued by the state government because he was visiting on official business.[26]

The piece of paper that he brought with him that day was a school record issued by the state. As overseer of School District Four, the state required Adolphus Sherburn to count every person in the district between five and twenty years of age, and he intended to do just that.[27]

When he came to the Conner homestead, an interesting conversation must have occurred. Having their children recorded, with their race labeled, would have brought the state down on Elizabeth, William, Himebrick, and the other parents who were determined that their children should be treated as equal citizens. But that did not seem to be Sherburn's aim. We don't know how the decision was made, but a course of action had been agreed on by the all-white, all-male school board, a decision that Sherburn was to make clear to these newcomers: their children were accepted and invited by the board to go to school, and the board would attempt to do everything in its power to protect their children from the scrutiny and judgment of the state government.

Adolphus Sherburn must have stood in the doorway of the Conner cabin and told them all this and then taken down the names of the children who were at home. There was little

John Conner, age five, the only school-age child of William Frank and Elizabeth Shepard Conner. Then there were the children of William Frank's father, William Bright Conner, who was now widowed and remarried to Abigail. Cordelia, at twelve years old, was the youngest of William Bright's children from his first marriage, and she now had a six-year-old half brother called Alexander. Finally there were all three of Himebrick Tyler's motherless sons, Octavius, age eleven, Cornelius, age seven, and Jimmy, age five. Together these children made up almost a third of the school-age population in District Four.[28]

What must those parents have thought as they watched Adolphus walk away? They may have stood outside their cabin watching, knowing their children's names were neatly written on the folded piece of paper he carried with him, watching his pale form moving through the close trees until it disappeared into the unceasing green. What a risk they were all taking that day. Courage, trust, and faith had to be held together hard, by both sides.

No one can say how powerful Adolphus Sherburn's visit was. The paper he filled out still exists in the state archives in Lansing, with the names of all the children on them, but he designated no race to any of the children, protecting the illegal children in his charge through the sin of omission. Soon after he came by the Conner land, the Cass County group made their move, literally, deciding to integrate not just the school but the entire township.

A family of lumbermen from Massachusetts named Packard was looking for good timber to feed the old mill they had just bought in Covert. Rich in pine and other valuable trees,

William and Himebrick's land was extremely enticing, and the Packards offered them a goodly sum for it. With that money William and Himebrick were able to buy rich farmland. William and Elizabeth bought land on the south side of the township, near where the Packards lived. (William's father stayed behind, however, more than happy with his forty acres and a school.)[29] Himebrick Tyler bought eighty acres near the village and settled there with his new family. Somehow, he and the widowed Louisa had met, maybe through Nancy and Joseph's encouragement, and in 1868 they were married. Himebrick was thirty-five, and Louisa ten years younger. Himebrick, the man who loved children, was now the father of six. He and Louisa would have six more children, their noise and laughter probably helping them to turn their backs on the loss that had marked the ends of their earlier marriages.[30]

William Jones, a twenty-year-old African American man who had been born in Michigan, gives an indication of just how rare an opportunity Covert's schools were for people of African descent in the Midwest. He arrived in Covert with his father sometime in the late 1860s. William was a second-generation Midwesterner, for his father had been born in Indiana, but just because they were both born and raised in the North did not mean that they had had access to education, and neither father nor son could read or write. William had three younger siblings, ages thirteen, ten, and six, and when they started attending school, he made the extraordinary choice to join them. He was almost certainly older than his teachers, the vast majority of whom were still in their teens, but he was willing to sit with children in the rough log cabin to learn what he had never been able to before.[31]

The school board had to use many ways to protect its black pupils, particularly since Lansing was still expecting school reports. Before 1866 the reports had been full of detail; after 1866, when the first African American children successfully integrated into Covert's school system, the reports dried up. They were sent, but only the bare minimum of information was given — where the schools were and what the school budget was. Covert's school board had a secret, and they were keeping it safe in the most honest way they knew — by keeping quiet.[32]

By omission and understatement the leaders of Covert began to carve out a secret oasis of acceptance. In 1863 they reported that "the condition of our district library is good as far as they go and we are well literate and well read for a new settlement."[33] In fact the school library collections held almost two hundred books, an enormous amount for a frontier community. Covert's citizens had made the extraordinary decision to spend what was then a small fortune to buy these books in 1856.[34] The purchase had cost the township $160 at a time when a man could expect a day of his hard labor to earn him a good wage of $1, and it meant that Covert had almost a book per person in its collection, at a place and time when many felt lucky to have a single Bible the entire community could share.[35]

The residents of Covert were also an incredibly literate group. Ninety-nine percent of the settlers above the age of five could read, and what they were reading was amazing.[36]

Many of the titles in the collection are long forgotten by readers today, books such as *Life of Josephine* and *Dr. Dick's Celestial Scenery*. Others are more familiar, such as the works of Edgar Allan Poe, the published papers of Henry Ward Beecher, and novels by Herman Melville. But virtually the entire collection would have been familiar to the residents of Covert, for the books would have been read aloud to their children at school, read at home by parents, and passed from reader to reader until the bindings cracked and the pages tore. These books almost certainly shaped how the residents of Covert thought about the world, their nation, their neighbors, and themselves and are powerful indicators of how they were thinking about race.

While the works of Henry Ward Beecher are commonly known to be sympathetic to abolitionist causes, other books in the collection were even more radical. The romantically entitled *The Lady of the West; or, The Gold Seekers* was a deeply subversive text. It was written by a young man by the name of John Ballou and was published in 1855 in Cincinnati at a time when Ohio was known to be home to many abolitionists (including Harriet Beecher Stowe). In the introduction, Ballou professes himself a "Republican" (in sentiments rather than politics) who wrote the book "for the great American Nation."[37] In reality Ballou was a radical abolitionist who not only believed in freedom for all but also in civil rights and integration for all.[38] While the main theme of the story involves young men, their search for gold in California, and the fate of their loved ones, it ends with them finally settling in a community in Indiana. This community is the focal point of the book, and in describing it, Ballou makes his strongest arguments for integration — not just integration, but the right of all men, "of any color," to vote.[39]

The last chapter is a story within a story of a poor Irish Catholic widow by the name of Mrs. Boswell who manages to make it to Indiana with her family, only to have her children confronted with anti-foreign and anti-Catholic hatred at school. This, in turn, convinces her that education should be separate for different religious and racial groups so that they would no longer have to tolerate one another in the classroom.

Looking for answers, she goes to the home of a man whose neighbors call him an "Infidel" for questioning the rulings of the church on issues such as slavery. His name is Mr. Howard, and he immediately starts criticizing Mrs. Boswell for trying to start a separate school for Catholic children. He argues,

"To divide the schools! Don't you see that it is making the harmony in society still less? . . . Turn little children together; will they know any difference in creeds? No; it's taught to them by their catechizing parents, that's it. But the more the law separates their interests, the more will they separate themselves in feeling. The law ought to set the example of love, familiarity, and equality among the people. It is only by this union and noble tone of feeling and acting that we can ever expect to discard the horrors of slavery. Why, I have heard ministers make the inhuman assertion that persons of certain color, blood and birth have not the same rights as other people! And they tell me that this is religion! God forbid that old Howard or any of his family ever become guilty of believing in such a system of religion! It's disgusting!"[40]

The disgust of the "Infidel" has an effect, and Ballou goes on to describe how the community manages to be a place where neither "color or blood" was of consequence for those choosing to settle within the community, for "they claimed that God did not intend land to lie idle when so many men in different parts of the world had no homes." He adds, "neither would they [the residents] admit that God was foolish for giving man a desire to maintain his own rights and equality!" He ends by writing that this stance "has not been without producing its effects upon the people. Their children, black and white, native and foreign, associated together, and loved each other!"[41] These were haunting words from a book in use in a community that was soon to see black settlers arriving.

Another novel from Covert's collection was even more overt in its abolitionist arguments. *The White Slave* is a fictional account of a slave, the son of a Virginia "aristocrat" and his "concubine."[42] Written by Richard Hildreth, in 1836, *The White Slave* went through a number of reprintings and directly influenced Harriet Beecher Stowe when she wrote *Uncle Tom's Cabin*.[43] Hildreth's book was tame, however, in comparison with Harriet Beecher Stowe's radically abolitionist novel *Dred: A Tale of the Great Dismal Swamp*, which Covert also had in its collection. Like Ballou, Stowe criticizes the American clergy for its stance on slavery.[44] One of her most chilling characters is the Calvinist Mr. Jekyle, who kidnaps a freed slave and her children. When he attempts to sell them into slavery, the abducted mother kills her children in order to keep them from being enslaved. But this is not primarily a tale of black victims and passive suffering. Written after *Uncle Tom's Cabin*, *Dred* was less sentimental and more radically abolitionist than its predecessor, as it was created in response to the violence and turmoil surrounding Kansas in the 1850s. Instead of an "Uncle Tom," the hero of the book (Dred) is overtly modeled after the slave rebellion leader Nat Turner.[45] Two of the other main characters in the book are modeled after Frederick Douglass and Sojourner Truth, neither of whom could be described as submissive.

Like Ballou's book, Stowe's novel ends with the characters happily ensconced in the North, indeed as far north as Canada, where they live in freedom in an integrated community. When it was first published, in 1856, the novel sold more than a hundred thousand copies in its first month of sales. Its incendiary tone was deliberate, for while *Uncle Tom's Cabin* was meant to convince the South of the error of its ways, *Dred* was written to raise the passions of the North against the South.[46]

These books, available to the children of Covert, encouraged whites to see blacks, and blacks to see themselves, as heroes and heroines as well as recipients of a legacy of rebellions, reform movements, and daring escapes that both races participated in. And the integrated schools complemented the stories the children read by creating a unique sense of community identity as well as a proud identity for African American children in Covert.

Although the school on William Bright Conner's land had already been integrated soon after the group from Cass

County arrived, when Himebrick Tyler moved to a piece of land closer to the village of Covert, the integration process had to start all over again in that new district. The village school was new, the first to be started near what the local leaders hoped would be the town center. Previously the school had been a small horse barn, loaned by a Mr. Allen for a more educational purpose. Although rough, it was located near the community's only general store and offered a much-needed service to almost thirty children who now lived in the area.

The teacher was Eva Rood, who had recently arrived with her family from Massachusetts by way of Glenn, Michigan. While some of the teachers at the time were local, in these early years of settlement most were from out of state. Indeed, in 1870, when only five active schools existed in the township, Eva was one of three teachers from out of state, the others being Mary Marshal from Ohio and Kate McMellan from Scotland.[47]

Eva's family moved as one with the Packards, for they were all in the lumber business. Eva was young, still in her teens, but her parents had made sure that she had a decent education, and Covert's school board must have been delighted when she accepted their offer to teach at the newly formed school.

Her students were faced with rough wooden benches, no desks, and a few holes cut into the logs to shed some light. Eva sat on the only chair, behind a table at the front of the class, with a small container of flowers set before her.[48]

One of the first tasks Eva had her students do was to pick leafy branches from the nearby trees to cover the rough windows in order to keep the flies out. Unfortunately, the cows

William Conner's farm, 1892. William Conner was a respected politician and one of the wealthiest and most powerful African Americans in Covert.
Portrait and Biographical Record of Kalamazoo, Allegan, and Van Buren Counties, Michigan (Chicago: Chapman Brothers, 1892)

Myrtie Conner, one of William Conner's youngest daughters, c. 1890. Her elder siblings integrated Covert's schools. Private collection of Ernestine Carter Taitt

The Teachout Homestead, c. 1880. The Teachouts came to Covert from Ohio in the 1870s. The Teachouts' log cabin and log-strewn land were typical of new settlers struggling to survive in Covert. The economic disparity between blacks and whites during the 1870s could well have led to rifts between the races, but this decade saw William Conner winning the powerful position of Covert's justice of the peace.   Covert Museum

The Tyler Family, c. 1895. Himebrick Tyler walked from North Carolina to Michigan with the Conner family before the Civil War. He is pictured here with his second wife, Louisa, whose first husband died in the Civil War. Sitting, from left to right: Louisa, Gertrude, and Himebrick; standing, from left to right: Julia, Sheridan, Elvira, Minerva (Himebrick's niece), Myra, Sherman, and Arvena.   Private collection of Ernestine Carter Taitt

Napoleon Pompey, 1880s. This Civil War veteran would have been in his late forties when this photograph was taken. By this time he was the wealthy owner of a seventy-nine-acre farm and had held political offices in the township. The pin in his lapel may well have been attesting to his membership in the Grand Army of the Republic.   Covert Museum

Washington and Annis Pompey and their children, c. 1900. Washington Pompey, a black Civil War veteran, organized and supported Emancipation Festivals in Covert. By this time Annis was a successful businesswoman, owning Covert's only cider mill.   Covert Museum

Covert road-building crew, c. 1900. When Dawson Pompey was illegally elected to the position of highway overseer in 1868, he would have managed an operation like this one. Although this photograph dates from 1900, the techniques used to build roads in Covert had not changed much since the 1860s.
Covert Museum

Paulsville School, c. 1900. Although having a school photo taken was obviously a difficult endeavor, involving shouted directions from the camera operator and large flash explosions, members of the more newly arrived Phillips family mingle in easy intimacy with their white classmates. The boy who would grow up to be Pearl Sarno's father stands at the front with his dog.   Covert Museum

Covert school photo labeled "Townline School, Packard Station," c. 1900. Despite the rise in segregation across the country because of the growing strength of Jim Crow laws, Covert's schools continued to be integrated. Covert Museum

The Lamson and Rood Fruit Packing Company, with the town of Covert in the background, c. 1900. By this time Covert was a well-established community whose economic base had shifted from lumbering to fruit growing.
Covert Museum

A Covert peach-canning and -packing crew, c. 1900. Although none of the members of the crew are named, Elvira Tyler is almost certainly the woman seated on the left side of the porch. She is one of at least five African Americans working in this integrated group.   Covert Museum

Allen Pompey's Livery Business, 1898. The African American Allen Pompey was Dawson Pompey's nephew. In the early 1870s he had come to Covert from Indiana, where he had been assisted by William Packard. By 1898 he owned Covert's only livery, on the main street of town.
Willard A. Norton, *W. A. Norton's Directory of South Haven, Casco, and Covert, 1898 to 1900* (South Haven, MI: W. A. Norton, 1898)

William Packard, c. 1880. Packard was a Yankee lumber baron and abolitionist who was the patriarch of the mill-owning Packard family in Covert. He made sure that the logging camps and mills he managed, as well as the church he built, were integrated. *History of Berrien and Van Buren Counties, Michigan* (Philadelphia: D. W. Ensign and Co., 1880)

Sunday school class of 1893. Frank Seaton, son of Joseph and Nancy Seaton and nephew to William Conner, stands second from the left. Frank Rood stands in the center, sixth from the left. His heavily bearded father, Edward Rood, who had come from Massachusetts with the Packards, sits in the center, third from the left. J. R. Spelman, standing at the far right, would later interview the Conner family about their walk from North Carolina and publish their account in a local paper.

Sixteen Sunday schools were started by the Covert Congregational Church in 1890. The Sunday schools met in members' homes, and at least seven of these groups had African Americans attending, sometimes in such numbers that they made up a third of those in attendance. Covert Museum

Covert Congregational Church Ladies' Group, c. 1910. This may well have been the same group of women who put on the fund-raiser for the Covert Colored Band in 1880. Although none of them are named, many of them were almost certainly pioneers in Covert's frontier days and instrumental in shaping Covert's integrated culture. Covert Museum

Group of friends from Covert, October 1896. Many of these young women had become friends in Covert's integrated schools. They continued to be close into their early twenties. Ora Seaton is on the far right, second from the bottom. Her friend Gertie Enslow is seated in front of her, wearing a plaid dress with sleeves so large her friend Gilpha has to pull them out of the way in order to see. Alice Adams, the daughter of a black Civil War soldier from New York, sits at the center of the group, holding the document they all seem so interested in.   Covert Museum

Tyler Sisters, c. 1890. No names are given, but they are almost certainly (from left to right) Julia, Arvena, and Elvira. In 1890 they would have been nineteen, twelve, and fifteen, respectively. Arvena's autograph book survived to leave a record of her many cross-racial friendships. Private collection of Ernestine Carter Taitt

Page from Arvena Tyler's autograph book.
Private collection of Ernestine Carter Taitt

Covert high school dance, c. 1955. By this time Covert's population had changed, and many of the African Americans now living there had come north with their families in the 1920s. While schools across the rest of the nation were scenes of violence, Covert's culture of integration continued.   Covert Museum

Pearl Sarno teaching her class, Covert grade school, 1959. Pearl Sarno's father had grown up in Covert, attending one of its many integrated one-room school-houses. She was first a teacher and later the principal of Covert's elementary school. Pearl Sarno founded the Covert Museum, and through her extraordinary efforts the community's unusual history was preserved.
Covert Museum

that wandered loose around the neighborhood found the leafy screens a tempting sight and would eat them, and Eva long remembered the commotion caused by a cow tongue winding its long pink way through the window coverings. Maybe she joined her students in their laughter — after all, she was barely out of childhood herself.[49]

The children she taught were truly a diverse group. Some children's families had lived in Covert for years before she arrived, like the Hawks and the Tripps. Others had just arrived from out of state, like the Shaws from Ohio. And then there were all the Tylers, both Himebrick's and Louisa's children.

As with many reminiscences, Eva's memories, written down in the early twentieth century, are tinged with nostalgia. Still, the ease with which she recalls the children she taught, along with her consistent lack of mention of race, is astounding for a woman who had lived through the rise of Jim Crow in America. Yet, for all of her warm memories of her early years in Covert, Eva was clear that life was a challenge on the frontier. Acceptance and integration did not happen because life was easy in Covert. Many of the white children she taught were of the first generation to be born in Michigan. Their parents had made up the motley group of settlers who welcomed Elizabeth and her group from Cass County. They had felled the trees to make meager clearings and hauled the logs up for the building of shelter, and when night fell they sat inside the darkness of their rough cabins, their faces lit only by the gleam of firelight.

While the group from Cass County was focusing on having their children integrate into Covert's schools, the Pompeys were going after an even bigger prize — political power. But first they had to hack out a homestead. The Pompey brothers had bought good land between Himebrick's and that of Levi Friend. Levi was much like them: young, single, and eager to succeed, famous in the township for the outrageous act of buying a piece of precious plate glass to create a window he could see through — the first of its kind in Covert. The four young men, three black, one white, saw a great deal of one another as they struggled together to survive.[50] As Himebrick later put it, we "lived near each other, came into a new country and worked much together aiding each other."[51]

The Pompeys' intention for one of their family members to gain a political position was a bold one. This was a time when even well-known and respected African Americans could not ride unmolested on a train out East. Just a few months earlier, Harriet Tubman, who had survived so much before the war, was riding a train in New Jersey when she was dragged by a conductor and his three aides from her first-class seat and thrown with such force into the baggage car that she was injured.[52] If whites would do this to a famous black woman, one could only imagine what retribution could be wreaked on an unknown black man demanding not just equality but power.

That man would be Dawson Pompey, Washington and Napoleon's father. Once they had assured their father that they had found a community where Dawson could make a good home, he moved from Whitley County, Indiana, leaving behind his brother Fielding, with whom he had survived untold trials to become the free landed farmer he was.[53] Dawson's farm in Indiana must have been a valuable one, for he was able to buy what was widely considered the best piece of farmland in Covert, a 160-acre homestead near the village that was one of the only cleared pieces of land in this frontier community.[54] To create cleared land was no mean feat in heavily timbered Covert. For many years the air was thick with the smoke of the burning trees that settlers, desperate for open fields, set alight where they had felled them. When the earth could finally be broken under the plow, it was black from the ashes of the forest that had once grown close around the farmsteads.[55]

By 1870 Dawson's land was worth $6,000. To put this amount into context: a few years earlier, in 1863, when the Conscription Act was passed to draft men into the Union army, a man who did not wish to fight would have had to pay a $300 bond, a lifesaving amount too large for many to afford.[56] In 1860 a male farm laborer in Michigan could expect a wage of around just fifty cents a day, and the average yearly earnings of a wage laborer in 1870 were $186.[57]

By 1868 Dawson and his extended family were well settled in their new home. Being on some of the best land in the township, Dawson was almost certainly taxed accordingly, and he had sons who had proven their title to citizenship by fighting for their nation, so Dawson decided to attend the local township election. His aim was not only to vote — an illegal action in itself — but to win a position in the township government. That was beyond illegal; it was audacious, particularly given the state of things in Michigan. In 1866 a man by the name of William Dean, from eastern Michigan, in what would become a suburb of Detroit, had attempted to vote in his township's election. To most, Dean looked white, but someone in his community knew that one of his ancestors generations ago had come from Africa, and he was arrested and sentenced for the crime of voting while only one-sixteenth black.[58]

In 1867, just one year after William Dean had been imprisoned for trying to vote, white Michigan voters turned out in vast numbers to vote against allowing black men to become full citizens.[59] Still, Dawson Pompey would not be dissuaded. The position that he wanted was a significant one — the position of highway overseer in his district — and he must have known that a white man already desired it. If he won, his duties would include gathering taxes from roughly thirty tax-paying members of their district as well as managing road-work.[60] That labor was supplied by the men of each district, who were required either to pay a tax or give a certain amount of time to building the roads. Since most frontier homesteaders were cash poor, the bulk of Dawson Pompey's work for the township would be overseeing a team of white men doing the heavy labor of chopping down trees, cutting brush, and leveling earth by hand.

April in Michigan is all muck, and Dawson must have been thinking of all the improvements he could make as he walked, almost certainly with his sons, to the cabin where the election was being held. All that bogginess brought forth great beauty, however. Dawson would have walked through an astounding array of wildflowers, so delicate that they would bruise if touched and never seemed to survive picking. In the early spring, when the chickadee first changed its call to courting, these tender green things would wake from their sparse and wild beds. Seeming to grow on nothing but sand and snow-melt, they covered the hills before the trees could block their light with leaves. Here were Dutchman's-breeches, perfectly translucent white hearts that did indeed look like opulent pantaloons worn by courtiers two hundred years before. And then there were the trilliums. Beds of these flowers could cover whole hillsides, rising six inches above the sands and bursting forth with double trinities of three dark green leaves that perfectly framed three sturdy white petals. Once in a rare while, there was a wake-robin, dark pink, almost red, a startling color next to the paleness of spring.

Towering over everything were the trees. Many were considered a nuisance, merely in the way of a good field for crops, but some were known to be more useful. Here in the cold north region, far from the sugarcane fields of the South, there was still a little bit of sweetness. In early spring, when snow was still possible, the sugar maples would begin to weep sap from the ends of their branches. Children soon learned to watch for the frozen drops to form at the ends of the lowest branches and snap them off to suck, the flavor weak and wild. The sap always rose after a night of hard cold, the sky clear, the stars seeming as far off as summer. But if that cold was closely followed by a warm sun, the trees would sense spring long before snowdrops would break their blooming way through frosty ground. Now was the time to bring out the buckets. If snow was still on the ground, the trees would leave a telltale spattering of sap all around them, the sweetness dripping from the ends of branches, with a force of rising so fierce the wood could not contain it. After all the rush and hurry of the rising would come the slow warm smoky work of rendering the syrup. The sap had to simmer for hours before its flavor changed from a tender bud green to heavy, brown, and sharply sweet.

After all the trees, and all the mud, came the men, walking to gather for decisions that would shape the direction of their community in this springtime of its settlement.

Although the Civil War had supposedly won freedom and rights for all black Americans, in a strange twist people of African descent were granted the right to vote in the former Confederate states by a federal government that could force the issue, whereas in many of the Union states, Michigan being one of them, civil rights had not been granted. However, just because blacks in the South had the legal right to vote did not mean they had the real freedom to do so. Many who tried to vote found their homes and crops burned or, worse, their persons and families attacked by murderous mobs. Heaven forbid they try to run for office; as an editorial in a Mississippi newspaper in 1869 so clearly put it, "Nigger voting, holding office, and sitting in the jury box are all wrong."[61] It is estimated that between the short period of 1868 and 1871, at least four hundred people of African descent were lynched in the South because, like Dawson, they were free and dared to think of themselves as citizens.[62]

Now Dawson was daring to do just that in Covert. Politics was one of the rare things that brought the residents of the township together. This is no metaphor. There were few reasons for the people of Covert to gather, outside of these township elections, and, realistically, no easy places for them to do so even if they wanted to. There was no church founded and no town hall built, and the schools gathered only the children from each district. It was one of these schools that hosted the elections that April. If it was one of the schools that was also a barn, there is a chance that the roughly eighty voters who gathered there that day fit inside its walls, but more than likely they milled about outside, while the township board sat inside the school. The clerk, with his pen and ink pot, would have been set up at the teacher's desk. There would have been little difference in the weather between inside and out, however, as any rough covering over windows and doors would have been removed to allow light into the building. As the men who came to vote entered the building to confer with the clerk and the board before the day's proceedings, they would have experienced an all too familiar blindness as they shifted from day to dim interior.

There is no record of how the votes were counted, only that the elections moved swiftly, which makes it likely that there was no secret ballot, only voiced intentions and a show of hands. The first vote was for township supervisor — seventy-seven votes were cast, and William Trafford won the close election with forty-two votes. The elections moved along; township clerk and township treasurer went without a hitch. Then came the vote for Justice of the Peace. That last position split the vote equally, with thirty-seven going to each man. This required some members of the board to "draw lots for the choice," and Briant Williams was finally declared the winner. While some men did not vote for these positions, all seventy-seven voted for the position of highway commissioner, for roads were of high concern for these settlers, many of whom, like Dawson, had to walk along muddy trails and over shifting sand hills to make it to the schoolhouse. Chester Bunnell barely won, with forty-one votes. Afterward a school inspector was swiftly voted in, as well as eight constables, whose job it was to aid the Justice of the Peace in his work.

Dawson and his family must have been mightily keyed up by this time, but finally it was their turn. The vote for the highway overseers was announced. The elections were held in order of districts, with James Tripp and Draper Fish winning their positions in Districts One and Two. Then came the surprise. Joseph Toquin, a local Pokagon, stepped forward for the position in the district where he lived. Most of those gathered there that day would have been aware that an "Indian," as he was later described in the voting records, had no right to vote, much less hold office. But then again, they all knew that the Pokagons were the primary residents of District Three, so it must have seemed only fair that he be allowed to oversee the work of his kin in creating roads in that region, and he was voted into the position. Only white men stepped up to fill in the remaining positions until it came to the last one, District Seven. This was the very district the elections were being held in, and it had one of the largest budgets, as well as the best equipment, for the township had just bought a scraper for the roads already built in this district. Now Dawson took his courage in his hands and stepped before the men who he hoped would continue to be his neighbors.[63]

Here he was, a relatively wealthy black man who, when he

had arrived in Covert, bought the only piece of cleared land in the township — a fact that must have still rankled some of the white homesteaders who were trying to eke out a living from the few bare patches of land they had been able to clear. And now he was attempting to break laws and social conventions by running for the position of highway overseer of his district, a powerful post previously held by some of the most prestigious white men in the township.[64]

Nevertheless, that day in April 1868, the men must have looked at Dawson and met his gaze, raising their hands and calling out their votes as the township clerk scrawled across his ledger page, "Highway District 7 — Dawson Pompey." They had done it — this motley crew of struggling pioneers from New York, Massachusetts, England, and Germany and the proud men of African descent who had made their way from the South and other parts of the Midwest were willing to do what so few were able to even consider — vote for a black man instead of a white man, breaking the boundaries of race and the law.[65]

As more people came to settle Covert, they had to learn to adjust to the new ways being created there. Those who did, however, continued to strengthen the ties created between the races.

For example, in June of 1869, Dawson Pompey bought a team of red oxen from a white man named Samual Jamison.[66] This may seem like a mild occurrence when blacks were being attacked across the South, but through such mundane interactions as these, an unusual community was being formed. Samual and his wife, Gertrude, had recently come from Ohio with their seven-year-old daughter, Maggie.[67] Samual needed money to start homesteading in Covert, and Dawson paid him fifty dollars for his ox team. Samual would have been well aware that Dawson owned the largest piece of cleared land in the township and had grown sons who were also landowning farmers. His transaction with Dawson, in addition to giving him the money to start his farm, would have had other value as well, as it created a relationship between a newcomer to the community and a wealthy, politically powerful farmer, who in this case happened to be black. Many Midwesterners would have found such a relationship intolerable, but Samual and Gertrude decided that this community was to be their home and that Dawson would be their respected neighbor. Similar decisions would be made by more whites as the township's population continued to grow.

Why? Why would blacks in Covert take such risks and make such challenges, and why would whites respect and encourage those actions? "Knowing one another" is not an answer in itself to why Covert occurred. During this very time a man of African descent in North Carolina was perceived as trying to gain too much control over his own fate, so he was dragged from his home in the middle of the night, stripped naked, and severely whipped by two white men he had been close with since childhood. The three of them had, in fact, been raised together. He never brought charges against them, however, for fear that they would kill him.[68] One of the many reasons why Covert occurred happened during this time of settlement, when whites and blacks first met and learned to know one another as equals, whereas the Southern black man had been thought of as chattel by his white tormentors.

But Covert was continuing to form itself, and in the coming decade the muck would persist and get worse in Covert, despite the best efforts of the road builders, for a logging boom was coming, and soon ancient trees would be felled and dragged to the massive mills that would spring up all over the township. Logging camps and mills were notorious for their lawlessness and violence, and the white men drawn to the labor available would be confronted by African Americans who were competing for the same jobs. In addition, both the black and white populations would double. This population explosion would strain the acceptance of the whites already in Covert and challenge the expectations of those who were moving there.

In the midst of all this turmoil, Covert's citizens would build a church, a town hall, and a general store. Clubs would be started, business would boom, and families would grow. And amid all these changes African Americans would make their strongest bids for power and continue to demand rights to education, legal justice, and social and economic equality. Anywhere else in the Midwest, these demands could have easily resulted in imprisonment, violence, or even death. But in Covert the ties between whites and people of African descent would grow stronger.

Chapter 4

Citizenship: 1870–1875

"Negro Manhood says, 'I am an American citizen.'
Modern Democracy says, 'You are not.' Negro Manhood says, 'I demand all my rights, civil and political.'
Modern Democracy says, 'You have no rights except
what I choose to give you.' Negro Manhood says, 'I must
build churches for myself, and school houses for my children.' Modern Democracy says, 'If you do I will burn
them down.' Negro Manhood says, 'I will exercise the
rights vouchsafed.' Modern Democracy says, 'If you do
I will mob and murder you.'"

— Benjamin Tanner,
The Christian Recorder, 1868[1]

It was November, and it was cold. William Frank Conner
huddled in his warm coat as his horse trudged heavily through
the sand, its hooves breaking through the light crust of snow,
leaving clear dark tracks behind him. Soon it would be winter
proper and the air so cold that every breath would bring with
it a sharp metallic tang, as if not just the earth but all the
world was hard as iron.

As William drew his coat closer round him, he remembered when Novembers were warm. It did not seem all that long ago that he was a child in North Carolina and snow a wondered-at rarity. And then there was the November of 1864, in South Carolina, where the fresh-spilled blood steamed in the dank morning air breathing off the swamps around Honey Hill. But that blood had been spilled eleven years ago. Now the only splashes of red William could see were the wintergreen berries that grew low around the trail he rode.

Unlike many seasons past, this November was a time of plenty. The harvest had been gathered, and the hogs left to run wild in the woods all summer had been slaughtered. A family of hogs had taken up residence beneath the floor of one of the schools, seeking the cool earth and shade there. Mostly, the children and teacher had become accustomed to the sounds and smells of the schoolhouse swine, but, still, sometimes the pigs caused trouble. Once, class had been disrupted when an older student grabbed a pig's tail as it poked between the wide gaps in the floorboards, making the animal scream in fear and fury.[2]

This was the time of year to prepare the meat, when it was cold enough to have the time to deal with all of it before it could spoil. Everyone was involved; even neighbors were brought in to assist, although it seemed that the women would always try to arrange for the help to be delayed a day or two between slaughter and smoking, so that some of the meat could be had fresh, the only time that they would enjoy that special treat.

William needed the aid of a couple of friends to dip a

heavy carcass into the boiling water in order to loosen the coarse bristles. Even so, it would take some hard scraping to get the hog white and clean. What a pretty sight it was when all done, ready to be cut up for feasting and smoking.[3] The winter cabins were now tinged with the smell of smoked meat from the hams and sides of bacon that hung richly from high hooks.

They would have more than meat to sustain them this winter. Like many of the cabins he passed on his way through the snowy woods, William's home would probably have had low lines of earth around it where perishable fruits and vegetables were buried under layers of dirt and straw to protect them from frost. In the months to come, his children could dig with mittened hands to reveal apples, red as gems and sweet as summer, buried beneath the snow.[4]

Just as bright were William's memories of the past few years. So much had happened, it was hard to believe that five years could hold it all.

There was the November five years ago, when all the men of Michigan had gone to vote, yet again, on whether to accept the Fifteenth Amendment, which would enfranchise William and his kind. The Covert voters had gathered in another little one-room schoolhouse to participate in the general election. The atmosphere must have been tense, for although two years earlier Dawson Pompey had won a position — illegally, by virtue of his candidacy and voting — no African American had run for office since. Approximately one hundred men voted that day, although only seventy voted on the African American suffrage amendment. The amendment was not uncontested —

sixty voted for the amendment, and ten voted against. Even so, William and all the other black people in Covert must have been grateful for the outcome. William, Elizabeth, and others almost certainly heard that the whites back in Cass County had voted against the amendment. Indiana, former home to the Pompeys and still home to their kin, would officially deny its black residents the right to vote for another decade.[5]

William now made his way through the chilly November woods to take full advantage of the right that was now legally his — he was on his way to run for office. And not just any office: he wanted the position of Justice of the Peace, arguably the most powerful position in the township.[6] This would not come as a surprise to those who knew him well. His wife, Elizabeth, had known for years of her husband's dreams and of the many trials he had survived in order to attain them. He saw no reason to reduce his ambitions because of others' perceptions.

Just because blacks were legally allowed civil rights, however, did not mean they got them, even in the Midwest. Earlier in 1875 a black man had been refused service and forced from a bar in Waverly, Missouri, based on the fact that he was of African descent. The man returned with a copy of the current Civil Rights Act and calmly read it aloud to the bartender who had treated him so poorly. As soon as he had finished reading the act, the bartender killed him.[7] Although William may not have heard of this event, in all likelihood he had heard of the Coushatta Massacre in Louisiana, which had occurred just a year previous, for it had been such a grievous occurrence that it had been covered by many newspapers. Six democratically elected white local officials — and their black supporters — were driven from their homes and shot by enraged racist white men.[8]

Even in South Haven, the town closest to Covert, an advertisement placed in the *South Haven Sentinel* in 1872 for the Pioneer Clothing Store showed a racist stereotyped depiction of a black man dressed in wild and fancy clothing who is announcing, "How am dis for High? Golly ain't I Style? I got my new clothes at Pioneer Clothing Store."[9] This in a township where the thirty-one African American residents made up only 1 percent of the population and most were day laborers; only one black family owned a farm.[10] While African Americans in Covert were able to achieve greater equality, economic success, and even political power than in other parts of the country, they would still have had to endure the reminders that many white Americans considered them unworthy of respect.

At the time a Justice of the Peace acted as both judge and jury in local civil and criminal suits. He oversaw a minimum of four constables to aid him in arresting offenders and keeping the peace and could also levy fines, marry couples, and settle local legal disputes. It was a position of real power and hierarchy; if William won, he would do so only with the support of many of the whites in his community.[11]

He would have the support of his whole family, now back together again. His sister Nancy was newly returned from Kansas. In 1871 she, her husband, Joseph Seaton, and their four little ones had set off for that new frontier. Ora, their youngest, had been only a baby, and the other three barely past toddling. They had headed to Lawrence, Kansas, home to a strong abolitionist community. Just eight years earlier, Lawrence had been the scene of the worst civilian massacre to take place during the Civil War, with almost two hundred people slaughtered by William Quantrill and his raiders. The Ohio-born Quantrill and his men had fought a guerrilla war against Union troops and sympathizers, but in the summer of 1863 he gathered 450 men and attacked Lawrence. In 1871 that Kansas community would have been still raw from the losses inflicted there, but the Seatons must have decided to add their numbers to the blacks already bravely living in Lawrence. It had taken the Seatons six long months to get there and about a year to figure that they preferred Michigan. Soon they were back in Covert.[12] Nancy almost certainly had missed her family, and Joseph had continued to struggle with the lung disease he had brought back from the Civil War.[13]

By this time word must have spread of Covert's culture of integration and equality. People of African descent were continuing to settle in Covert, their numbers now exceeding sixty, making up more than 8 percent of the population, and they were flourishing. (For a chart on the African American population in Covert, see Appendix page 219.) The Pompeys were responsible for some of this. Dawson and his sons had worked hard to persuade others of their family to join them from Indiana, and several had heeded the call, including Dawson's daughter Catherine, with her husband, Douglas Pompey.[14] Many of the blacks who came, however, were not related to any of those first families who had settled Covert in the 1860s. They came not for family but in hope of a better life. Many of them found it. None of the black-owned farms in Covert was less than forty acres, and together the lands owned by African Americans were valued at $21,600.[15] This was an extraordinary sum for a time when a farm laborer in Covert could expect to make $17 a month.[16]

Soon these landed farmers were being asked to join the newly formed Grange Society.[17] The Grange had been founded in 1868 by Oliver Hudson Kelley, an employee of the United States Department of Agriculture who, with the aid of other friends in the department, helped to create an organization that would offer friendship and support to farmers in a nation recovering from civil war. It quickly became enormously popular in Michigan.[18]

Like the fraternal organizations it was based on, the Grange joined its members together through secret rituals. These rituals created an intimate and strong bond among the members, and the organization soon fostered new friendships as well as business ties.[19] Although Grangers were often perceived as political agitators, struggling for their rights within a growing national marketplace, they saw themselves as members in a society that valued leadership and fellowship.[20] As an advertising pamphlet for the Grange put it, "Its members are largely property-owning people. Therefore dependable and stable citizens."[21] A member of a Wisconsin Grange in the 1870s stated that the most important goal of the Grange was "to prepare and encourage farmers to take leadership in society."[22] F. G. Adams, writing in the *Kansas Daily State Journal* in 1885, noted of the Grange, "Through this intercourse [provided by the Grange] many a Grange brother and sister has become conscious of acquired power, to think and speak more clearly; we have learned to divest ourselves of narrow prejudices, and have learned lessons of charity and good fellowship in all our relations with our neighbors."[23] A Grange required twelve officers, and their ranks could include women.[24]

The formation of a racially integrated Grange in Covert in 1873 was astounding for many reasons. First, in the South the Grange societies not only excluded people of African descent but were sometimes merely a front for the Ku Klux Klan. (This forced black farmers in the South to create a separate club for blacks called the Council of Laborers.)[25]

Although the South may have seemed a long way from frontier Michigan, the creation of a Grange, a branch of a national organization, in Covert is a powerful reminder of how connected Covert was with the outside world. Covert's radical race relations did not occur because the community was isolated and unaware of the racism so common outside its borders: Covert's decisions were made in the full knowledge of racism and in defiance of the norms accepted by many whites in the Midwest.

Not everyone in Covert was interested in farming, however. Maybe Joseph Seaton had tired of the plow, working on the plains of Kansas, because when he returned he went to work in one of the many sawmills that had sprung up all around the township. He still grew a few crops to help feed his family, but his bond was with wood and the men who worked it, and by 1875 there were a goodly number of such workers.[26]

The loggers who accompanied the local logging boom were known for their violence and lawlessness. (In the 1950s an elderly Covert resident remembered that his grandfather, who had been a logger in Covert in his youth, was missing the tops and bottoms of his ears, lost to some other man's teeth during one of the many fights he had gotten into at the logging camps.)[27] Each weekend these loggers would make their often-raucous presence known, and there must have been general chaos when they came to town from their outlying camps.

It may well have been the behavior of these lumbermen that persuaded William Conner to run for his position. Still, standing for election was a bold move on his part because more and more whites were flooding into the township every day, drawn by the economic boom fueled by the mills. With no knowledge of the unusual race relations in the community, and dependent on the mill owners for their jobs, these new settlers could quickly turn on any black man they saw as a threat.

All of the sawmills in Covert were owned by the Packard family, and by 1875 their holdings were worth an extraordinary one hundred thousand dollars. Even the local papers had begun terming Covert "Packard's settlement."[28] As noted earlier the Packards were accompanied and supported by the Roods, and they all hailed from the Berkshire Hills of western Massachusetts. Their village had been perched on the edge of a hill, and the land offered little to farmers, being not much more than thin soil over thick rock. They had briefly settled in Chatham, Ohio, close to the shores of Lake Erie, before coming to Michigan. Edward Rood, like the Packards, was a Congregationalist and a Republican. He was proud of the fact that he was of pure Puritan stock, his mother, Abigail Hawes, being a direct descendant of a Mayflower pilgrim. Edward had come to Covert with his wife, Flora, and his two young children, Frank and Lillian, and the Packards set him up in his customary position of foreman of the mill. But he had been a lumberman long enough to know all too well the boom-and-bust cycle of logging. Now the father of two young children, he was ready to settle down, and as soon as he could he bought two hundred acres and started a hardware and farm equipment store, for he knew farming would follow hot on the heels of logging.[29]

The Packards and Roods had been lured into the lucrative lumber business, and they had been slowly making their way west since the 1840s. With a steam engine and a good saw, a man could make a fortune from the trees that settlers were eager to clear off their land. A man could lose a fortune, too, and members of the Packard family had survived at least one bust before coming to Covert.

The Packards were formidable businessmen, but theirs was a formidable business. Others had tried and failed to attain the Packards' success. The first sawmill in Covert had been built by Samuel Paul, in 1857. His business lasted long enough for his little patch of industry to be called Paulsville, but by 1859 the operation had been abandoned, and the infant Covert had its very own ghost town on the shores of Lake Michigan.[30] Ten years later another attempt was made, this time by Hawk and Lambert. Their enterprise fared even worse than Paul's, lasting only a few months.[31]

A mill's success or failure depended not only on a steady source of logs but also on a volatile market. If farmers in Nebraska lost their crops to locusts, they would not demand wood for new barns. If officials in the British colony of Guyana decided that their first choice of Michigan pine was too expensive, they might turn to their jungle's own wood. If the winter was a warm one without sufficient snow and ice, it would be impossible to move the logs from where they were felled to the mill. And if conditions were excellent, the market could become overwhelmed with wood.

William Packard was the patriarch. Born in 1808, in Plainfield, Massachusetts, he grew up in Chatham, Ohio. There, he married and later started a successful lumbering business. By the time he was forty-eight, he was a wealthy man, the owner of five sawmills. Then he lost everything in the panic of 1857 and left Ohio, moving to join his sons, who had started a sawmill in Allegan, Michigan. In Michigan, William and his sons were able to make a go of it. But lumbering is a short-lived business; when the trees are gone, so is the money. After ten years in Allegan, William and his sons got word of relatives in Covert who had managed to buy not only a mill but a great deal of good timberland. They moved west to Covert and added their investment and assistance to the operation. In just a couple of years, they built two more mills, turning Covert into a boomtown.

William Packard and his sons were certainly drawn to Covert for financial reasons, but there were family concerns as well. Alfred, William's nephew, who was running the operation in Covert in 1870, lost his wife, Laura, in that same year. Laura and Alfred had been married for eleven years, and she had traveled with him all the way from Massachusetts. Their baby son lived only five months after Laura's death, leaving

Alfred alone and grieving. William could have offered both aid and sympathy to his nephew, because he had lost his own wife seven years earlier and had lost children as well.[32]

Despite their setbacks, the Packards made it a priority to stand firm by their faith and their beliefs, both of which were more than a little radical. They were abolitionists, believing in freedom for all. The Packards' native Massachusetts had been a hotbed of abolitionism by the time they left to seek their fortunes in Ohio, and they may well have been influenced by radicals such as William Lloyd Garrison and Frederick Douglass, who were converting many to their cause across the nation. Soon after arriving in Chatham, Ohio, in the 1840s, the Packards had found a church after their own heart and ideals, a Congregationalist church whose young minister, Stephen Peet, was of the new generation of abolitionists — unwilling to wait any longer for the abolition of slavery and unwilling to tolerate anyone, Christian or otherwise, who defended the cause of human bondage.[33]

Peet almost certainly allied himself with the American Anti-Slavery Society, which had been organized in 1833. The abolitionist William Lloyd Garrison wrote the group's constitution, which included the society's top two goals: the total and immediate end of slavery and, just as important, the removal of racism so that people of African descent might "share an equality with the whites, of civil and religious privileges."[34] The young abolitionists who backed the cause of black freedom and parity realized that one of their first challenges in persuading other whites to end slavery was to convert their minds and hearts away from racism and toward an acceptance of blacks as fellow "brothers" and citizens, deserving of equality and justice. Once this was accomplished they hoped that slavery would quickly end.

In aiming their energies toward black equality and citizenship, this new generation of abolitionists had turned their backs on the often racist rhetoric of the American Colonization Society, who were opposed to the very presence of people from Africa in America. For years they had been trying to free slaves in order to send them to Africa.[35] While technically abolitionist, they were still often virulently racist.

By the early 1840s Congregationalists, Presbyterians, and even the Quakers had been torn apart by differing notions on how and when to take a stand against slavery.[36] Around this time the Reverend Stephen Peet decided to write a new charter for his church in Ohio. Taking his cue from the many abolitionists in his region who were becoming increasingly intolerant of placating slaveholders, he wrote,

> We regard slavery as it exists in our country a great sin against God and our fellow men. . . . Against our fellow men as it deprives them of the invaluable privileges, social, civil, and religious. . . . It deprives them of the unalienable right which God has given them of life, liberty, and the pursuit of happiness. . . . And we resolve that . . . we cannot admit a slave holder to officiate in our pulpit or to participate in our communion.[37]

The statement's strong language angered many of the members of the church, who quit in protest. But the Packards held firm, backing Peet and supporting him as he continued his radical ministry. They would continue to hold firm when they came to the Michigan frontier looking to make a fortune from the stands of virgin timber that covered the land. They had no church there, but they would have been well aware that the Michigan Congregational Church, upon its first general association meeting, declared itself strongly pro-abolitionist, and its members began actively working to end slavery in the nation.[38]

Now, however, the war was over, and many abolitionists had lost their fervor for their previous ideals in the wake of the strife and bloodshed that had so recently ended. The Packards, in a way that was both radical and at the same time old-fashioned and conservative, obviously held to their old prewar beliefs. The Packards had known that blacks lived in Covert; some of the first men they had done business with in Covert were black. Soon it was known that the Packards were willing to hire black laborers in their sawmills, and the subsequent population explosion brought on by the jobs available in the mills was racially mixed, spurred by their unusual hiring practices.[39] Moreover, Covert's mortgage records reveal that the Packards' assistance had gone well beyond hiring. A pressing need for settlers of any race was currency. In this cash-poor society the economy was based on barter, but there were times when only cash would do, and buying livestock was one of them. The Packards soon became known for their generosity and willingness to make loans to those in need, no matter what their race.

In early June of 1872, Ichabod Packard, an early settler of

Covert and a distant relative of the mill-owning Packards, was approached by Allen Pompey, one of Dawson's nephews who had come from Indiana to join his uncle.[40] Allen Pompey brought with him his wife, Huster Jane, who most everyone in the township, including the census taker, assumed was white — making him doubly dangerous to racists.[41] But even with all these strikes against him, Allen Pompey had dreams of becoming a businessman. He knew his horses and wanted a career in which he could work with them — maybe a livery business on the main street of the small town. But even if he was able to overcome the challenges of entrepreneurship, his success alone could endanger him. It was not unheard of in the nineteenth-century Midwest for successful black business-men to be shot as they stood in their own front yard or to be run out of town for competing with white businesses.

But just like the rest of his family in Covert, Allen Pompey was not hindered, and by 1872 he was doing so well that he decided to expand his farmsteading operations with the addi-tion of a milk cow and a pony. He knew that Ichabod Packard was looking to sell some livestock, and in June of 1872, Pom-pey approached him with an offer. Ichabod agreed to sell Allen a red cow and a pony for about fifty dollars — quite fa-vorable terms. Allen then asked if he could owe Ichabod the last thirty dollars until harvesttime, in the fall. Ichabod agreed to this request, and they decided to meet in the hall above the general store, where township business was often conducted, to have their agreement signed and witnessed by the township clerk.[42] Neither the Packards nor the Pompeys could know that in twenty years' time Allen Pompey would become the wealthy and successful owner of the community's largest livery stable on Covert's main street. All they knew was that race should not define a man's dreams or hamper his potential.

By 1872 the Packards could afford to be generous. They had successfully turned Covert into a world of raw wood and smoke. Early settlers must have laughed at their memories of burning valuable lumber in order to clear the land for farming. Now the smoke in the air was from steam mills fueled by the wood dust created by the giant saws. Before steam power it had taken two men — one in a pit below the log and one above — walking along the length of the log, pushing and pulling the blade through the wood and working for hours to slice a single tree. Now one mill had a seventy-two-inch, steam-powered upright saw that could cut through close to a mile of wood a day. Although steam-powered saws were faster and easier than the old process, they were still immensely dangerous. They would not stop if a hand, leg, or body slipped into their sharpness.[43]

The Packards' mills and others like them around the state had made Michigan the nation's leading lumber producer, outstripping the two former leaders, Pennsylvania and New York. This meant, however, that the lands and forests of Michigan were also subjected to unchecked ecological destruction. Some areas saw only a decade of prosperity before the trees ran out, leaving behind a desert of blowing sand interrupted only by stumps. These were not the only remnants that logging left in its wake — dead and dying boomtowns also dotted Lake Michigan's coast.[44] Some early settlements, such as Singapore, about twenty miles north of Covert, rivaled

Chicago in the 1840s. But even this bustling port town was deserted by the turn of the century. There is no trace of it now, its homes and mills slowly buried under a wrath of sand that the inhabitants of the town had loosed from its green bonds.

At the height of the boom, the forests were being cut at such a rate that the Packards kept all three steam mills running, and as many as three ships a day took the cut wood out into Lake Michigan and beyond. The Packards had gotten around the problem of the dunes that had bested the previous mill owners by building an elaborate railroad across them, so that horse-drawn carriages could carry the wood to the shore. No dunes were leveled for the railroad; instead, the wagon drivers would gallop their horses down the slopes to gather momentum for the next rise, like an industrial roller coaster.

The railroad ended at the rough edge of the dunes, and there the Packards built piers that jutted three hundred feet into the water. The laborers would have stood at the end of them and watched the big boats sail in from Chicago and Milwaukee with nothing but wind and horizon behind them. The shoreline sloped so slowly that even at the ends of the piers the water surrounding them was only about eight feet deep, and it took great skill to navigate the heavily loaded boats alongside and then away. Their captains, and those working on the docks, would have to hope for calm waters during the six hours that it took to load the vessels, as Covert could offer no harbor and no protection from the storms that could come and splinter ships against the massive pilings.[45]

The Packards' mills produced at least three million feet of

lumber a year, which in turn produced sawdust that had to be shoveled up and thrown into the furnaces of the mill. The furnaces could not keep up with the amount of sawdust created, so it was gathered into mountains that covered more than an acre. These hills of wood waste smoldered and occasionally erupted into flame from the heat created by their mass. On windy days the wood dust was blown about like unmeltable snow, drifting under doors, settling on hats and hair, and tasted in every breath.[46]

In those days, as in ours, business was based on credit, and a business the size of the Packards' required a sizable line. This meant that the Packards fell under the intense scrutiny of credit agents as far away as Boston. R. G. Dun, based in Massachusetts, had thousands of agents in the field, from the muddy streets of Manhattan to the mountains of Montana. Agents would track down the friends and enemies of the applicant, from ministers to business partners, from family members to bartenders. A favorable credit rating could be won or lost based on one's reputation, and good character, in the nineteenth century, was a fragile and valuable thing. One's social life, marriage, drinking patterns, and friends were all fair game. Once credit was extended, reports continued to be gathered, and a loan could mean having one's character and personal habits scrutinized for years. For over a decade the Packards were the subject of more than twenty reports. R. G. Dun knew when the Packards got married, when a son broke off to start his own business, when a mill burned down, and what their customers thought of them. But at the end of each report, like a chorus, ring the words, scrawled in the R. G. Dun shorthand, "gd hbts, gd ch," which translates as, "good habits, good character," words worth their weight in gold. They were "number one men."[47]

And William Frank Conner was running against one of these "number one men," for the position of Justice of the Peace.

There were other men like Conner in southwestern Michigan making similar claims to power. In 1872 William Hardy, a farmer who was the son of slaves, won the popular vote to become the Gaines County supervisor. Gaines County was some sixty miles from Covert, but his position was one of such extraordinary power that word of his win may well have reached Covert. What made Hardy's triumph all the more unusual was the fact that his electorate base was almost entirely white and pronouncedly Democratic in their politics. At this time the Democrats were a party passionately opposed to black civil rights. There are no clear answers to Hardy's win, although Hardy, unlike Conner, was very light-skinned. But looking like a white man was not enough to protect William Dean when he had wanted to merely vote just six years earlier. Perhaps, at the height of Reconstruction and with a slight warming in the relations between whites and blacks in the Midwest, the white men of Hardy's community had been able to see the common ties between themselves and this successful farmer.[48]

William Conner may also have been encouraged by Napoleon and Washington Pompey, who, following in their father's footsteps, ran for and won positions in the township in 1874. While Washington chose to run for highway overseer, like his father, Napoleon had successfully pursued a far more dangerous position as constable. Consequently, if William won his bid for Justice of the Peace, he would be overseeing an integrated band of constables.[49]

In 1868 Dawson had gone to the local school to declare and stand for his position. Now Washington, Napoleon, and William gathered in a more formal space above the general store, a hall used for any town gatherings, from the Grange meetings to church. The hall was the creation of the Packards and was called, aptly enough, Packard's Hall.

The Congregational Church service that took place weekly there had been formed by the Packards and the families that had come with them from Massachusetts. The creation of the church was one of the first public moves the Packards had made when they settled in Covert in the late 1860s. There was a service held on the first day the congregation was formally organized and recognized as a church. The Packards invited Stephen Peet, their old abolitionist minister from Ohio, to give the sermon on that special day.[50]

Once the hall was built, services were held there. The hall was large but would have still made for close quarters when all the worshipers gathered, the women's large skirts pooling around them in cascades of calico. In the warmest days of summer, everyone must have longed for the dark, high-ceilinged coolness of a real church.

That long-awaited church was also being underwritten by the Packards, who were donating their finest lumber for its creation. It took a decade to finish, finally opening in 1878.

Now, however, Covert's hall was playing its part as a place of politics, not a place of worship. Sitting in Packard's Hall, a sea of white faces surrounding him, William Conner must have thought of the closed white faces behind the bulwarks of Honey Hill. This vote would change his life, just as that battle had. He hoped his neighbors would accept his challenge gracefully and that his actions would not endanger his life or the lives of his young family.

The other two men running, Ichabod Packard and James Mererry, were both white and they were both seasoned politicians. Of course the Conners and the Packards were no strangers to each other. The Packards had bought timberland from William Conner soon after arriving in Covert, and William's brother-in-law, Joseph Seaton, worked in a Packard mill. And not only was William running against a Packard, if he won he would be the boss of a Packard, for Alfred Packard was a township constable.[51]

William Conner had at least two supporters who would almost certainly have been encouraging him as he sat in the hall waiting for the election to begin. Any member of the township, of any race, first needed two men to sign an oath and give a five hundred dollar bond to guarantee that the person elected would perform his duties well and honestly.[52] Five hundred dollars was a powerful sum of money in a day when fifty dollars could buy a cow and a pony. This meant that, long before he ran for the election, William had to have met with and been guaranteed the support of two men who were willing to bond him to the position if he won. These two men were so sure of William's abilities that they had underwritten his bid for office.

The hall was packed with voters when the clerk read aloud the results of the election.

One vote for James Mererry.

Eight votes for Ichabod Packard.

One hundred and thirty-six votes for William Conner.[53]

William must have almost choked as he was pounded on the back by his supporters, his hand wrung by delighted voters. Their man had won.

And afterward? William could rest easy, knowing at long last that he had the power to protect those he loved and punish those who would harm them. It was too late to help his aunt, who had been stolen away from him when he was a child, but he must surely have been thinking of her as he walked out of Packard's Hall into the cold night. He would have mounted his horse, probably still surrounded by well-wishers. As he set off, he must have glanced back more than once at the well-lit hall, his neighbors still gathered outside talking over the events of the evening, events William was almost certainly eager to share with Elizabeth. Even at night in the thick woods, the dark tracks of his journey there would have cut clear and sure through the snow, showing the way home.

Chapter 5

Equality: 1875–1880

"It was a very interesting community. Some of the finest people of New England blood, some of the finest Negroes, some others including Indians were there."

— Eva Carnes,
born in Covert, 1876[1]

By 1877 the last American troops had left the South, marking the official end of Reconstruction, leaving the newly freed black population to face the tender mercies of a white population who had not wanted them to be free in the first place. The withdrawal of federal troops from what was essentially a simmering race war zone meant that there was little protection for people of African descent from those who longed for revenge. Letters sent North carry the pain and desperation of this period, for this was backlash in its ugliest form, a backlash against a usually defenseless population. A black lawyer in South Carolina recorded some of the horrors, explaining, "While I write a colored woman comes and tells me her husband was killed last night in her presence by white men and her children burned to death in the house; she says her person was outraged by these men and then she was whipped — such things as these are common occurrences." He then begged those he was writing to, "in the name of God," to help him and his fellow blacks leave the area, for "Africa or some where else where we can live without ill treatment."[2]

If only he had known of Covert. During this time, far from the struggles unfolding in the South, Covert was booming. Every day more and more people arrived to settle the land and work in the mills. Yet for all the opportunities Covert afforded, it was still an odd community. Here were religious, teetotaling Yankees, deeply accented Europeans, Indians still walking the deepest woods, and Pilgrims' descendants, all trusting their businesses and safety to black men who policed and judged the community from lovely homes on rich farms.

What caused the new settlers to accept such a different way of being? For some the issue was not acceptance at all. People of the nineteenth century, although perceived as living in simpler times, were not simple people. Those moving to Covert were not blind to its culture of equality — some even focused on it. Those men and women, blacks and whites, who came to Covert did so either because they cared sufficiently about living in an integrated community or because they had no interest in expending energy on efforts to promote racism. Certainly the economic opportunities Covert offered were a tempting trade-off for accepting an unusual community culture, but it was also the community culture itself that allowed people to accept this way of life. Covert's belief in integration and cross-racial cooperation was welcoming to both whites and blacks, meaning that a white family newly arrived in Covert could be offered assistance by its black neighbors, or a black laborer could be offered not only a job but shelter by a white family.

Even more important, Covert's relatively young culture of radical racial harmony was by now widely accepted by the older, more powerful settlers — including new arrivals — who seemed deeply invested in its continuation. Pioneers of African descent were eager that the equality they had helped to establish persist and strengthen so that their children could know a way of life that their parents appreciated as rare and valuable. Every school district in Covert that held African American children was integrated, as were the other township institutions. The Packards and their generation of abolitionists often held the belief that racial equality should go hand in hand with the freeing of slaves. Now they may well have been trying to live out their beliefs. So while those of African descent continued to actively seek more integration and equality, the most powerful whites in the community actively encouraged their actions. The result of all this was that Covert's unusual culture not only blossomed but bore good harvest, while the rest of the nation saw the meager fruits of Reconstruction wither on the vine.

But in 1876 Edwin and Elizabeth Gillard knew none of this. All they knew was that they had to move south. Both were Canadian, born and bred, but they were determined to head south, where the growing season was longer and the winters less deadly.

So they loaded their life onto a barge. Everything that could go was going: the furniture, the cart, a cow, the children, the axe, the clothing, and themselves. This was to be no lazy trip along slow canals, but a rough and difficult one, pulled behind a steamship on Lake Michigan. They intended to go to Indiana along the length of the lake.[3]

Edwin and Elizabeth were better off than many settlers, with an ox team, a cow, and the money to hire a boat to tow them, but the journey south did much to destroy their fortunes, for Lake Michigan is a risky body of water. Historians argue over just how many boats have been swallowed by this inland sea, but no one disputes how brutal the storms on the lake can be, how quick they can come up, and how big a ship they can sink. When a storm did arrive, the Gillards' barge had little chance. Then the worst happened; their barge was ripped from the tug that towed them, and they were adrift in the awful shove and heave of the water. For Edwin and Elizabeth there must have been the terrible moment when the truth hit — the wet deck of their wooden barge could quickly slip off the edge of everything into nothing that was solid anymore.

Watching a piece of wood in the surf, slowly washing back and forth for hours before beaching, gives an idea of the agony experienced by this family as their wreck made its wretched way toward the shore. The high forested dunes would have been visible throughout their journey, but once adrift in the storm, the land could only tempt them, a seemingly unreachable safety. Once ashore (who knows who vowed it first), they were home, never to travel again.

Their barge saved them twice, first from the lake, then again when its logs were turned into the bare bones of a hut for that first terrible Michigan winter. "That first winter was very hard on them . . . they lost some children" is how the family records read. Elizabeth, a small woman by all accounts, went out to the woods with a five-pound broadaxe and felled the trees that would become the main timbers of the house, her axe hacking deep into the flesh of the wood to form beams that would hold a roof to shelter her remaining children. Her grandchildren would later look up at those beams in wonder at each broad bite into the wood the grieving woman had made.[4]

Elizabeth Gillard's black neighbors may well have heard the sounds of her axe, and they may have come to meet their new neighbor and offer help, for with their integrated settlement pattern, there were few places in Covert where a white family could settle without having a black neighbor nearby.[5] Neither the Gillards nor any of the roughly four hundred other whites who settled in Covert during the 1870s could escape the fact that they lived in an integrated township.

While many of these new white settlers were struggling to survive, they would have also been aware that many blacks in Covert were, on the whole, quite wealthy. Of course there were newcomers who came to labor in the Packard mills or start a homestead, but the Pompeys, Conners, Seatons, and Tylers had now been joined by the Russels, Jacksons, and Shepards, and their wealth was astonishing. Blacks had refused to be relegated to a particular region of the township; instead, they picked the land that would support them and their families and lead them to prosper. Their strategy worked. Not only did they own good land, they owned better and more valuable land, overall, than whites in the township. What exactly did this mean? It meant that though whites owned more land on average than blacks (mostly because of the Packards and their hundreds of acres of forest), black acreage was worth more than double the value of white land, $47.23 per acre as compared with $19.43 — an astounding difference. (For charts on black and white land ownership in Covert, see Appendix pages 220–222.)[6]

Farming may seem a foreign and nostalgic way of life today, but in the 1870s the vast majority of Americans lived on farms. Owning a successful farm was central to gaining independence and success in rural America at that time — and that is just what Covert's black farmers were able to do. Their successes, independence, and economic power were exactly what most threatened racist whites.[7]

Indeed, a black man's success could endanger him, even in the Midwest. In the late 1870s a successful black businessman from Cincinnati, Ohio, shared with a friend that racism "hampers me in every relation in life, in business, in politics, in religion, as a father, or as husband."[8] A black lawyer of this period noted that when racial tensions arose in a community, it was often the most prominent and powerful black men who were at risk, for "the tallest tree . . . suffers most in a storm."[9] What a joy and a relief it must have been for the Conners, Tylers, and other successful black farmers to have their successes met not with hostility and hatred but with acceptance.

Part of that acceptance may have been won because of the generous aid offered by these black farmers to their white neighbors. After building a home the next step to survival was a barn, and building a barn was hard and difficult work, requiring the skill and labor of many. Both blacks and whites came out to help "raise" barns for their neighbors. Residents called these gatherings barn-raising bees, and whole families came out to watch the men fit the beams together and raise them high. A "bee" gave a good excuse to gather, eat, and celebrate the creation of a true homestead. There would have been an edge of fear, as well, when the men put up the bones of the barn, for great danger was involved when the massive wooden frames were pushed carefully into place using long poles. Lorenzo Pompey, one of Dawson's sons, was all too aware of that danger: during the raising of his neighbor Henry Vanarker's barn, an entire crosspiece section fell on him, permanently damaging his shoulder.[10]

The Pompeys took part in these bees, and they also gave food to new white settlers who had not had a chance to clear their lands yet. One of Washington Pompey's granddaughters remembered how the newly arrived settlers, who were often struggling, would come up from the valley near their farm to get food from her parents, who had a surplus to share.[11]

These warmly remembered stories of generous and kind assistance could be seen, from a more cynical perspective, as selfish and fearful. The elite blacks could merely have been trying to protect themselves from the resentment of poor whites. The anthropologist Marcel Mauss, whose groundbreaking work on the use of gifts to tie together communities and create cultures is still referenced by scholars today, would have taken one look at these warm and fuzzy stories of aid offered to newcomers and snorted in disgust. Through his eyes these helpful neighbors who often broke the boundaries of race to assist one another were merely self-serving individuals attempting to grow their community and protect themselves by "gifting" newcomers with everything from labor to food in order to persuade them to become good neighbors and to bind them into the community.[12] But if Mauss and the cynics were correct, there would have been many more communities like Covert. Lorenzo Pompey, for one, had lived long enough in Covert to know that the real risks he took in helping to raise his neighbor's barn far outweighed any resentments he may have experienced for refusing to help. And most poor Midwestern whites would have been horrified at the idea of taking charity from their wealthy black neighbors. The sad truth was that most Midwestern whites were strongly against having black neighbors, no matter how helpful they might have been. We cannot know how many whites chose to not even try to settle in Covert because of its unusual race relations, nor how many left soon after arriving, unable to tolerate — much less welcome — its unusual race relations. This was still a time of choices for many in America. There was still a frontier farther west that was open to homesteading.

If blacks had been the only ones helping needy white neighbors in Covert, Mauss may still have had a point, but help and welcome were offered regardless of race. Most whites who made Covert their home must have chosen to do so, for there would have been no way to avoid the integration and equality that were the norm there. And Covert continued to welcome new black residents; in the previous decade their numbers doubled from around fifty to more than a hundred, making them 9 percent of the population.[13]

One of those who found shelter there was Robert Penellon. Although Robert did not have to fight the lake to survive his journey to Covert, as the Gillards had on their barge, his arrival on Covert's shore was just as miraculous. He was young, single, black, and most likely a recently freed slave from Kentucky, the state where he had been born. He was also lame, his ability to walk hampered by some incident in his past. The most chilling reason an ex-slave would limp was because he had been "hamstrung," his muscles severed at the back of the ankle to keep him from ever running again.

Robert may well have heard of the job opportunities, available to any man, in the Packard mills, but his injury, not his race, would have seriously hindered his chances in an industry that required great skill and strength. It would have also made his journey to Covert slow and painful. Nevertheless, somehow he found himself at the door of Allen and Hannah Fish, around the late 1870s. What happened then was truly extraordinary.

The Fish family was well known in Covert. Allen Fish had come from New York with his parents in 1854. Allen was married to Hannah, although he had been a widower when he met her, and a good deal older than she was. His first marriage had been oddly famous, as it was the first legal union between two people of European descent in the township.[14]

Allen and Hannah were the parents of Arthur, a teenage boy whose energy was almost certainly channeled into labor on the farm, as his father was not able to work as much as other men because he was constrained by terrible scars, the remnants of burns he had received as a child. Maybe it was recognition, not race, that Allen and Hannah sensed when they first met Robert. Here was someone who also suffered from a difficult body. Even so, their actions were unusual even in Covert, for they invited Robert to work on their farm as a boarder.

Settled residents in Covert had long been offering their homes to boarders, but during this period of the logging boom, farming families who took in boarders from the mills might rely on them for a source of cash income to supplement the trade in goods from their farm.[15] There was a strict definition made between boarders, servants, and farm laborers. Boarders often had occupations such as teacher and mill worker, both wage occupations that allowed them to pay the family who fed and housed them. Only rarely did they barter their labor for room and board, yet this seems to be the arrangement that Allen and Hannah offered Robert.[16]

By making the decision to board Robert, the Fishes were also choosing to have a young African American man share their home, share their meals, and share their lives.[17] But Robert also had to make a decision. He may have experienced this kind of intimacy with whites when he was a slave, but now he was free, and it was his choice to live with Allen, Hannah, and Arthur, just as it was their choice to welcome him. Together, they made their decisions, freely, and by 1880 Robert is listed in the federal census as a "boarder" with the Fishes, working on their farm, eating at their table, and sleeping in their home.

Had Robert in his wanderings chosen a different community or a different state in which to make his inquiries as to a job and fair treatment for a good day's work, this story could well have ended very differently. In Rush County, Indiana, for instance, a young black man much like Robert came to the door of a farmhouse to ask for a drink of water. His name was William Keemer, but, unlike Robert, he would not have thought of himself as a stranger, for he had grown up in the neighboring community of Beech. Beech was an African American settlement that had been in existence for almost fifty years by the time William came to the door of the farmhouse in 1875, and at the time there were three hundred people of African descent living and farming there. The residents of Beech had long had close associations with the Quakers who lived nearby, but every day whites who were even openly hostile to their black neighbors were settling around them. The farm that William stopped at may well have been home to such a family. It was owned by the Vaughns, and Lucetta Vaughn was home alone when William Keemer came to the door to beg for a cup of water. According to William, when she saw him on her doorstep, she panicked and became hysterical. William, worried by the response, left, but when Lucetta's husband returned, she claimed that William had forced his way inside the house and raped her. The residents of Beech defended William. They had known him all their lives, and they hoped that their standing in the community could protect the young man. Two days after William had dared to ask for that cup of water, he was brutally lynched. Some claimed that the lynch mob cared little whether Lucetta or William was telling the truth; what enraged them was that a young black man had dared knock on the door of a white home asking for anything at all.[18]

While Robert and the other African Americans arriving in Covert integrated into the rapidly growing community, Covert continued to shelter a people who were intent on self-segregation — the Pokagons. Surprisingly, the Pokagons had managed to hang on to their land and now had their own community within the township of Covert that the other residents unofficially knew as Toquin, named for the most respected Pokagon family. There, they were able to keep their language alive and practice their lifeways.[19]

Despite the sawmill's hungry maw, there were still patches of forest in the wettest of the swamplands, and there the Pokagons hunted game and gathered food. They proudly stated the "uncivilized" nature of their lives when the federal census taker came knocking at their doors, forcing him to write "picking berries" in the occupation section of his modern and quantifiable records.[20] Toquin and his family were home when the census taker came calling, but few of his neighbors were caught for the count. These were a people unwilling to be pinned down and wary of being recorded by any government officials, as well they should have been.[21]

Yet the Pokagons were not unknown to the more recent settlers of Covert. No matter how well they managed to hide themselves from the people from foreign lands, foreign diseases often found them. While the Pokagons had better remedies for the ailments of America than any schooled doctor did, they were often defenseless in the face of the most common ailments from Europe.

It must have been a terrible desperation that drove Wesaw Mota to George Carnes's door, late one night. George Carnes was Covert's first doctor. He was in only his early twenties when he and his wife, Lucy, had arrived from Vermont a few years before.[22] Carnes may have had to answer the door in his nightshirt, but Mota lost no time, briefly introducing himself and then urgently telling Carnes that he had a sick child who needed immediate medical attention. Wesaw quickly added that, unlike many of the doctor's white patients, he could pay for the doctor's services, with a "little pig."

Carnes would not have known at that moment that he was talking to one of the oldest Pokagons living in the township. Wesaw Mota's "child" was almost certainly his grandson, Bosile, who was living with him and would have been about six.[23] Wesaw and his wife, Mary, had bought land from the federal government in the mid 1850s and had raised their family in Covert.[24] Their elder son, Samuel, lived nearby, with his wife, Elizabeth, and their six children. Their younger son, Thomas, lived with them, along with his wife, Mary Ann, and their little son, who was now terribly ill.[25]

Some of the most popular books of the period were those that told tales of tricky and bloodthirsty savages and of the women and children whom they kidnapped and killed. Covert's library was not exempt from this racist literature, making it easily read by any of Covert's citizens.[26] But after following Wesaw into the night woods, Carnes returned safely to his family and went back to Wesaw's home many times to bring Bosile through his fever.

George Carnes may have been able to help Bosile Mota,

but there was much he could not do, including help his wife when it came time for her to give birth to their first child — that was women's work. Eva had been born shortly after he and Lucy had arrived in Covert. Eva was rocked in her mother's womb for weeks as they made the long trip to the new settlement. Wealthy William Packard's wife must have heard of Lucy's need, and when the birthing time came, she arrived to aid Lucy, helping her "as one's mother would."[27]

Although the nineteenth century saw the construction of rigid social norms, women in rural America at that time (which means most women) lived a life where the division of labor between domestic and public existed much more in theory than in practice. Of course women were denied a role in the most public sphere of life — politics — but where the physical and economic stability of their families and farms were concerned, they were extremely active. In addition to raising children, their tasks could also include caring for much of the livestock, including chickens, cows, and pigs, as well as making bread and butter and sewing all the family's clothing. A day would often start with the cow complaining loudly, letting everyone know that she needed to be milked. Once milking was done, there were the chickens to check on. This was always a worrisome duty, as it seemed that any number of weasels, possums, foxes, snakes, raccoons, and other predators could squeeze themselves through the smallest crack in the henhouse wall and cause carnage. If the birds were alive and well, then it was time to collect the eggs from underneath the warm and sleepy hens. This was a treat on a chill morning, the downy belly of the chickens radiating warmth. Unfortunately, this joy was brief, as the shortening days of winter left the hens molting, and with their shed feathers came a lack of eggs that would be sorely felt by the family until spring.

Aged chickens, their laying days over, were gratefully used in other ways. Once eggs could not be procured, there were meat and feathers to be had. (A feather pillow was much preferred to the more common alternatives of straw and corn husks.) But first a chicken had to be killed, and a neck is a hard thing to get through. Some women simply used a hatchet and chopping block; others mastered the quick trick of the twist, wringing the chicken's neck before it had a chance to become overwrought.

All this came at a price, for all through the winter everything still needed to be fed and, worse yet, watered. If there was a pump, then water could be had, but it did not stay liquid long. The watering tins full of ice had to be struck against the barn wall to dislodge the discolored blocks that stuck so stubbornly, or the buckets might be left to melt by the woodstove, where the ripe smell of whatever had been drinking from it would fill the home. But this hard work translated into real and necessary income for the family. Surplus eggs and butter could be taken to the store in the village and traded for fabric, coffee, sugar, and other goods that could not be raised, grown, or made.

This was work done by women in farms across the Midwest at this time, testimony to the fact that in many ways life in Covert was typical of a rural Midwestern community. Of course markedly uncommon were the community's race relations, though by the late 1870s, Covert had managed to work a wonder — they had made even this exception seem normal. This was probably one of the most powerful reasons why all the new settlers to Covert were able to accept the way things were: integration and equality had become utterly conventional.[28]

Many scholars feel that the most interesting histories happen during those moments of violence that reshape institutions, but some feel there can be something thrilling about a community that works hard to keep things the same, to preserve a radical status quo, *despite* the many changes within a community, such as new settlers arriving.[29] And while things were changing inside Covert, they were also changing outside it. Blacks across the country and their sympathetic white counterparts were deeply troubled by indications that the nation and her leaders were turning their backs on the promises they had made to black citizens, both in the North and the South. Reconstruction was being blatantly attacked and weakened in the South, and in the North whites were growing less interested in defending the civil rights of blacks, both in the South and in their own communities.[30] A black intellectual in Illinois, troubled by what he was seeing around him, wrote, "There is a feeling all over this country that the Negro has got about as much as he ought to have."[31] Many whites felt that not only had the "Negro" received enough, he also had probably received too much.[32]

Even in Covert there were some troubling incidents that indicated things could be changing. In 1879 nine white men decided to start a secret fraternal organization, the Independent Order of Odd Fellows (IOOF).[33] Anyone starting a lodge was required to follow its rules, and its rules clearly stated that "no person shall be permitted to be a member of any Lodge unless he be a free white male."[34] Blacks were not the only ones excluded. In order to be a member, one had to be employed (making a "good wage") and have been a resident of the region for at least six months. These guidelines excluded many of the men and women who were arriving in Covert to make it their home.

Fraternal organizations were highly visible within small communities such as Covert and a powerful means of creating hierarchy. There were literally the outsiders and the insiders, and the insiders — the members — shared a bond of inclusion. Not that everybody wanted in. The IOOF's member list was secret, so it is difficult to know who belonged to it, but the Packards, the Roods, and other powerful Yankee families who had founded the Covert Congregationalist church belonged to a religious organization and a generation that was rabidly anti-Masonic.[35]

Just a year before the IOOF was created in Covert, those Congregationalists finally had a real home. The new church was a lovely large structure, right across from Packard's Hall on the main street. It was modeled directly on its mother church in Chatham, Ohio, which was itself precisely modeled on the Congregational church in Plainfield, Massachusetts.[36] As these churches were replicated on a physical level, their builders' old abolitionist culture was re-created on a community level.

The year of the IOOF's founding in Covert, 1879, was also an election year, and William Frank Conner was running to be reelected as Justice of the Peace. His position was the most coveted in the township, and four white men put their names in to run against him.

Though four were running against him, the race was really between William Conner and Hiram Fish. Hiram was the father of Allen Fish, and he was a force to be reckoned with. He was an early settler of the township, arriving in 1854, and he still lived on the 320 acres he had bought at that time. As a nineteenth-century commentator on Covert wrote, "Fish soon became prominent in the affairs of the township, in which he was deeply interested." Interested, indeed. His cabin was the site of the first official township meeting, in 1856. Soon thereafter, he was voted in as one of the first township supervisors, the highest post in the community.[37]

In the end, Conner lost to Fish by only 5 votes, with Fish receiving 104 and Conner 99. The other three white candidates split the remaining 6 votes.[38]

William Conner may have lost his position, but he had not lost his power. Around this time he started gathering with other wealthy and influential black citizens of Covert and the surrounding area to plan a series of new and radical actions. They had proven they could run for office, their children attended the local schools, and their farms were profitable, but they wanted more: they wanted recognition. Years later American civil rights leader and intellectual W. E. B. Du Bois would grasp exactly what their aims were when he wrote that the "history of the American Negro" is the struggle to merge his uniquely African identity with his American identity, to be able to be "both a Negro and an American without being cursed and spit upon by his fellows, without having the doors of Opportunity closed roughly in his face."[39]

William Conner and the other blacks in Covert had walked through the door of opportunity, but now they were intent on having their own unique heritage and identity celebrated. A white-only fraternal organization had been created? Then they would create their own fraternal society and limit its membership to men of African descent. The nation was beginning to turn its back on the rights of blacks? Then they would insist not only on equality, they would insist on recognition — they would create a festival that would be so big and so lavish that the whole region would know of its existence and know of their proud heritage.

For years the blacks of Covert had been integrated, sharing equally in the life of their community, but now it was time to separate, it was time to be recognized, it was time to be celebrated.

Chapter 6

Independence: 1880–1884

"Black is not a color despised by God or man. Four-fifths of the human race are black. Black appears to be the favorite color with the Lord for humanity, and is a favorite color with man everywhere else except in the human face. . . . But it is not the color that is despised, but it is despised in this country because it has become a badge of poverty and ignorance. If it were a badge of wealth and knowledge how different would be our standing in the North. . . . What we want is not another color but power."

— Eugene Hardy, Emancipation Day speech,
Grand Rapids, Michigan, 1883[1]

This speech, given by an African American community leader in a city only sixty miles from Covert, by the 1880s was not uncommon for the time or region. By then African-descended Americans had for decades been creating festivals that celebrated their unique identity. These celebrations were known as Freedom or Emancipation festivals, and they were often held in early August to commemorate the end of the Atlantic slave trade in 1808 and Britain's emancipation of hundreds of thousands of slaves in the East Indies on August 1, 1834.[2] Such festivals traditionally involved parades, large gatherings, and, most important, speakers. The speakers would give rousing orations on the evils of slavery, the value and glory of people from Africa, and the rights those people deserved to have. The gatherings were attended by blacks and whites, and speakers of both races addressed an integrated audience. Those in Chicago, and across the Midwest from Ohio to Illinois, were famous.[3] No wonder that William Conner, Himebrick Tyler, and the Pompeys desired to start such a festival in Covert.

Some of the best-known celebrations occurred in northeastern cities such as New York, Philadelphia, and Boston, but by the early 1860s at least 150 Freedom festivals were being held in more than a dozen states, many of them in the Midwest. Not surprisingly, they met with opposition. In the 1820s the participants of the Boston Freedom festival had been so frequently attacked by whites that they changed their parade routes to try to avoid confrontation. After this failed they decided to protect themselves by carrying arms in the parade. In one famous incident a black Revolutionary War veteran, wielding his musket, single-handedly held back a mob until police could come and disperse the hostile crowd.[4] Years later, in 1876, Hamburg, South Carolina, was the site of violence. The local black community there had decided to celebrate July Fourth with a parade of their own soldiers. The black men marched in full uniform but soon were stopped, and some of those gathered were arrested on charges of hindering the flow of traffic. By the time they were brought to trial, more than a hundred angry whites had gathered. When the black soldiers refused to admit they had done any wrong, violence broke out. The whites had armed themselves, but the soldiers were now defenseless, having had their guns removed when they were imprisoned. In the end a number of the black men whose only crime was trying to celebrate Independence Day were shot and killed by the white mob.[5]

After the Civil War, "Juneteenth" festivals, held on a "teen" day in June, became popular. These festivals celebrated the American emancipation of slaves, the news of which did not reach enslaved Texans until June 19, 1865, more than two years after Lincoln declared slaves in America free.[6] (In its denial Texas was in bad company: because it was a Union state, Missouri was exempt from the Emancipation Proclamation and kept thousands of people enslaved throughout the Civil War.)

Both before and after the war, these festivals were widely covered by the black press, and it is possible that the Conners, Tylers, Seatons, Pompeys, and other African Americans in Covert subscribed to such papers and received word of the festivals in cities of the North and Midwest.[7] Then again, the Pompeys were in a position to have firsthand knowledge of Juneteenth, as their regiment's last assignment had been a post in Brownsville, Texas, where they could well have helped spread the word of freedom.[8]

Those of African descent who started the festival in Covert chose the first of August as their day to celebrate. It is probable that the festivals started in the late 1870s, and by the early 1880s the event was well enough established that even those outside Covert desired to be involved.[9] This was the rich, warm time of year, when everyone could afford to celebrate, when there was not just enough, there was too much: too many peaches, their soft skin turning blue with mold in cellars. Too many cherries, too much corn, and too much heat. The only escape from all of this was Lake Michigan, where the water was cool and there was always a bit of a breeze. Near twilight, one could wade out into the shimmering sea and watch tiny fish silently spring from the water, their splashes making it appear as if a magic and local rain were falling from a cloudless sky.

Even the nights were hot, and thick with sound. There were the insects who clicked and whirred through the still evening air, and then, on the dampest nights, especially following a good rain, there were the tree frogs, whose mating call was oddly musical, half-croak, half-chirp. Their eggs, housed on leaves, had to be positioned just so, over water, to ensure that when the tadpoles hatched they would drop right in, instead of drying and dying on the ground. Once grown they had to make their long trek up trees to start the cycle all over again. Like the residents that listened to them, they were a small and everyday miracle.

By August the frogs and leaves seemed the only green; everything else was gold. The grain, the corn, the grass, even the dust seemed a tired gold in the high heat. Soon it would be harvesttime, but there was still time for celebration, for hitching up the carriage, packing the picnic basket, and heading into town for a day of remembrance and rejoicing.

By 1881 William Conner, Himebrick Tyler, and the Pompeys had created such a large and well-organized event that when the city of Kalamazoo, forty miles away, had to cancel its festival at the last minute, those from Covert decided to invite everyone in Kalamazoo, as well as the neighboring city of Battle Creek, to their celebration.[10] This was a bold move on their part, as the summer of 1881 had already been an unsettled one. The shooting of President Garfield in early July had left many spooked.[11] Garfield had probably been a popular president in Covert. He was a Midwestern Republican and had been close to Lincoln, all-important factors for a Republican Midwestern community, where many of the men had fought in the war.

By late July of 1881, the president was still alive, though ailing, and William Conner, who with Himebrick Tyler and other black men from the region had arranged for the Emancipation festival, was determined that it would still occur, even if other communities had had to cancel theirs. To make it easier for those coming from far away, Conner and the others had already made arrangements to hold the festivities in South Haven, a harbor town near Covert that offered easy access by boat and train from Kalamazoo. About twice the size of Covert in 1880, it had only thirty African American residents, and none of them were land-owning farmers like those in Covert. Nevertheless, the whole community seems to have welcomed them.[12] They coordinated with the local train lines to put on a special service from Kalamazoo to South Haven and put out an advertisement in the local papers inviting all those in Kalamazoo to attend, giving detailed descriptions of the planned events, from music to steamboat excursions on the lake, as well as announcing that the ex–lieutenant governor of Michigan, Charles May, would be lecturing, in addition to "Prominent Colored Speakers."[13]

Their celebration, however, was on the defensive. A reporter at the South Haven paper wrote that "herculean efforts had been put forth by some of the neighboring communities to entirely kill off the observations of the day here." After this cryptic note, however, no more was said, so it is impossible to know to what lengths William Conner, Himebrick Tyler, and the South Haven men working with them had to go in order to preserve the day. But preserve it they did. On the morning of August 2, the train pulled out from Kalamazoo before dawn, filled with people. When it arrived in South Haven, its occupants disgorged into the already bustling streets. A local reporter estimated that by 10:00 a.m. more than twenty-five hundred visitors had arrived in South Haven for the festival.

Once there, the visitors gathered for the parade, which ended at "the grove," where there was a large picnic. Then the speakers came on, their themes hauntingly similar to those touched on by Martin Luther King Jr. at civil rights rallies almost a century later.

Although the festival had been under attack, none of its participants had ever been in danger of physical harm, unlike those who tried to celebrate in the South. Blacks in Covert may well have heard of this and other acts of violence against people of their kind in the South, and across the rest of the nation, for they were well connected to a broad network of civil rights activists and leaders across the country — so well connected, in fact, that they could call on some of the best-known figures of their day to come and speak at their festivities. The black leaders of Covert were literate men, who received and read black-published newspapers of the day, as well as traveled to Chicago and other major Midwestern cities. In 1884 they had speakers coming all the way from Tennessee and Ohio so that the residents of their community, both black and white, could be enlightened by these radical and righteous men.[14] One of the speakers in 1884 was the Honorable Judge John Patterson Green. Judge Green had a special bond with William Frank Conner, for they each had been the first black man in their region to win the position of Justice of the Peace, William Conner in 1875, John Green in Cleveland in 1873. Just a few years after being invited by William Conner to speak in Covert, John Green ran for and won the position of state representative. Later he went on to become a state senator.[15]

William had wanted particularly esteemed speakers to come to speak at the 1884 festival, for he must have been determined that that year's celebration would honor the memory of someone for whom emancipation meant so much. William had to send to the local paper both the announcement for the festival and the obituary for his dear Elizabeth's father, Henry Shepard, on the same day. Although Elizabeth had finally persuaded her parents to leave Cass County and come to live near her in Covert, in 1877, she had only seven years with them nearby before her father died. In coming to Covert, Henry Shepard, who had journeyed far and bravely to win his and others' freedom, had made his last journey.

Even though Emancipation Day symbolized the freeing of slaves, it was important for the African American residents of

Covert to remind themselves and their community that they were instrumental in that very act of freeing. Even though many of the participants in the festivities came from families who had been free long before the Civil War, this parade was a way for them to make a claim to a specific heritage and identity.[16] That heritage and identity was as people of African descent, shaped by their race but not bound by it.[17] In many ways the African American experience in Covert was a paradox. They had created, and were an integral part of, a community where the color of their skin made little difference to the wealth, power, or prestige they could gain. Yet the color of their skin had shaped their own experience before coming to Covert and the experiences of their ancestors, experiences that were unique to people of their race. Thus, though they lived in and shaped a community where the color of their skin did not define their social, political, economic, or cultural roles, they chose to create an identity based upon their heritage that was shaped by race. They would have been well aware, however, that though they proudly claimed citizenship not only of their community but their country, most residents of the nation would have judged them by the color of their skin alone — and found them wanting.

By marching in the Emancipation Day parade, William Conner represented the African American community, both in Covert and across the country, as a nation within a nation. But for William Conner and Himebrick Tyler, the real celebration would have come at the end of the day, when they saw what a success the festival had been. Their wives, Elizabeth and Louisa, probably clipped and saved the article from the

South Haven paper about the festival that noted, "All in all the celebration was a great success, and much credit should be given to Messers. . . . Conner and Tyler."[18]

The Emancipation festivities were an assertion of difference — a symbolic act of separation from the rest of the community. They were also, however, a re-creation of the ties between whites and blacks in Covert. Through this festival, blacks were making themselves an object of display, but through that display they were creating a proud identity that they themselves had constructed.[19] This was an astounding act of courage and self-awareness during a time when racist stereotypes and negative images of black people were increasingly common. The people of African descent in Covert were not content with equality; they demanded recognition. They did not desire mere acceptance; they insisted on celebration. And they were joined by prominent whites, such as the Roods.[20] The white citizens of Covert took the Emancipation festival seriously, even supporting it financially. Although the festival sometimes moved to neighboring communities, where it was widely written about in the local press, most often it was held in Covert. Covert had no paper, so fewer records exist for the festivals held there, but surviving documents make clear that Covert whites were intimately involved in the festival. It was recognized as one of the official holidays the town came out to celebrate, the other four being Thanksgiving, Christmas, July Fourth, and Memorial Day.

This recognition and support is in itself surprising, given all that the festival represented, and it extended beyond the holiday itself.[21] For example, on a high summer Saturday in the early 1880s, a group calling itself the Ladies of Covert put on a "Strawberry Festival and Social" to raise money for Covert's "Colored Band." The band played on many occasions, and it almost certainly performed on Emancipation Day. Even with bad weather threatening, the group refused to cancel. Despite the heavy thunderstorm rumbling outdoors and the oppressive heat within the hall, more than one hundred people, some from communities outside Covert, paid ten cents each to enter the hall to "partake of the delicious berries and cakes being served by the ladies of Covert." Lemonade and candy were also sold, "and as the weather was warm the lemonade was in good demand."[22] It was a chance to draw local bonds closer and also an opportunity for those from Covert to show off their integrated community. They were proud of what they had accomplished, and rightly so.

In other communities in Michigan where there were blacks and whites trying to share a life, blacks were asked to make many sacrifices in order for their presence and success to be tolerated by whites. In Monroe, Michigan, a mixed-race community on the shores of Lake Erie near Detroit, blacks had to deny their blackness, deny their heritage, deny their uniqueness in order to be tolerated by local whites.[23] There were certainly no Emancipation festivals in Monroe. Additionally, no whites were willing to vote for black suffrage in the state elections, much less vote for local African Americans to hold office. Yet the actual number of African Americans in Monroe in 1870 was 42 out of a total population of 5,086, making them only 0.83 percent of the population, a number that decreased to 15 by 1904.[24]

Three years after the founding of Covert's whites-only IOOF lodge, William Conner and his colleagues from Covert and nearby communities responded by creating their own segregated fraternal society, a branch of the Free and Accepted York Masons (FAYM). In January they held their first meeting in Packard's Hall, the same space that the white lodge met in. W. F. Conner, J. W. Jones, H. B. Tyler, Lorenzo Pompey, Benjamin Gowens, Edward Carle, William Jones, and G. Singer were listed as the charter members, and in little more than a decade, a local publication noted that "it has some of the best furniture of any in the state" and was "a prosperous organization."[25]

This was an extraordinary act of cultural division. In addition to flying in the face of those who had formed the IOOF, the creation of a branch of the Free and Accepted Masons made it clear to all of Covert that the township's wealthy and influential black citizens were an elite group in their own right. This did not mean that Conner and the eight black men who joined him in starting their lodge turned their backs on the ideals of integration. Instead, they continued to be involved in all their old associations, such as the Grange lodge and that elite fraternity of power, the political system.

For blacks, that realm of political power was, in reality, closely tied to the formation of a local black Masonic lodge. Across the Midwest, African Americans often belonged to one or more black fraternal organizations and used them as stepping-stones to leadership positions in local and state politics. William Conner, Himebrick Tyler, and the other more established blacks in the community may well have used their new lodge to prepare the newer black settlers to become community and political leaders.[26]

Before the next generation was ready, though, one of the pioneers wanted back in. By 1882 there were two Justice of the Peace positions open, one for a three-year term, and one to fill a vacancy. William Conner decided to run for the vacant position, which he won, and the following year he ran for and won a full three-year term. Conner's position was even more powerful than it had been before because now Civil War veterans in Covert were starting to apply for pension funds, and as Justice of the Peace, his signature was required on all Civil War pension applications.

Whether it was Conner's triumph or the close-knit fraternity that met in Packard's Hall that made it possible, within four years of Conner's reelection and the formation of the black Masonic lodge, three black men who had never run for office before, including Himebrick Tyler, ran for and won positions in Covert. Washington and Napoleon's younger brother, Lorenzo Pompey, their cousin Allen Pompey, and Himebrick Tyler all won positions as highway overseers, each in different districts. (For a chart on political positions held by African Americans in Covert, see Appendix pages 223–224.) As blacks were more and more frequently being forced into chain-gang labor in the South, often to do roadwork, white men in Covert were working on the same kinds of projects under the watchful eye of their elected black overseers.[27]

Not surprisingly, settlers who were not comfortable with Covert's unusual culture must have decided not to make the township their home. Certainly there were plenty of other places to go if one wanted to live in a racist community. This mobility was not unusual in itself. The township's more permanent residents had settled in many communities before finally choosing Covert, in a pattern that was common with many pioneers moving west at the time. Lumber-mill workers and logging men were a notoriously mobile group, prone to many comings and goings. But what of the people who insisted on making Covert their permanent home? Theirs is a different story, and not all of them accepted what was unusual about Covert.

One of those settlers was George Sternaman. In 1882 Sternaman and Conner had gone in together on a business venture. Sternaman was a young white man from Indiana who had just arrived in Covert with his wife, Minnie.[28] Conner was already a successful businessman at the time, and this may well have been his way of extending opportunity to a new member of the community. Whatever the reason, the two men agreed to rent ten acres of good cleared cropland from Henry Phelps, a local white farmer, to grow winter wheat. They agreed to share the initial costs and divide the labor. They also agreed that if their crop succeeded, they would split the product of it equally between them.

This was both a business agreement and a risk, for winter wheat is an odd crop. Once it is planted in the fall, it sprouts quickly, making the October landscape look as fresh and tender as spring. From then on it's anyone's guess whether the crop survives, for it needs a good heavy snow to insulate it from the freezing winds of winter. Covert, close to the lake, was prone to frequent and heavy snowfalls, particularly in the early winter, when Lake Michigan was relatively warm and free of ice. When the cold winds off the Great Plains hit the warm waters of the lake, the entire western side of Michigan was, in local parlance, dumped on. So theirs was a good gamble.

Sternaman and Conner must have kept an anxious eye on that field, particularly in that strange time after Christmas, when every year without fail when the winter seemed its strongest it would weaken into what is still called a January thaw. The warmth would last only a week or two, but it would be long enough for the snows to melt and for a few confused fruit trees to send some hopeful buds blossoming into the winter air.

This was a dangerous time for farmers, when feet of snow could disappear in a day and flooded fields could turn to sheets of ice overnight. But the sudden thaw also could make strange and beautiful things happen. The air, moist with melting snow, often created heavy frosts on every surface, so that the world seemed turned to lace, the delicate threads of ice extravagant, but sure to be lost soon after the sun touched them.

In the first few days of the thaw, the snow could melt so fast that it would literally steam up the warm night air, causing a low fog to form in the open fields. Moonlight would cause this fog to glow, the pale light reflecting off the still-white snow below, where it was trapped within the moist air. If anyone walked through such a night-lit cloud, it would be as if they were swimming through deep water, with little light and no direction.

After the thaw, winter always came back, clamping its gray helmet firmly over the dome of the sky, and soon all the world was snow again. By the end of March, however, the real thaw of spring was usually in full effect. The snow melted, but quicker than the soil, whose frozen firmness kept dampness from sinking through, so that there could be water everywhere, standing in pools and hollows, dark against the gray of fallen leaves. Once in a great while there would be a day of surprising warmth and sun, just long enough to melt the snow and cause the mud to spread, and then it would be bleak again. By the end of March the most common green seemed to be the new shoots of the tough wild roses that brambled their way up and out of the ground, climbing anything near.

Imagine, then, what a joy and a relief the winter wheat must have presented, standing up a smart two or three inches, the greenest thing around. The robust crop must have looked mighty good to the men who had planted it — too good, indeed, for Sternaman to want to share with a black man. Then again, the crop may have been poor; the problem would have been the same, with Sternaman deciding that his split was too small. Sternaman may have felt he had a stronger claim to the crop because he now lived on the land he and Conner were renting, and he may well have been encouraged by the landowner to make his claim.[29] Or just maybe this newly arrived white man held the belief that for all the indications of equality he had noted, in the end Covert would be much like the rest of the Midwest, where a white man could often do as he pleased to a black man and feel little heat from the law.

149

Could Sternaman really have been blind to the fact that, in Covert, Conner *was* the law?[30] Whatever his blindness or motives, we do know that on March 29 Sternaman came to the township hall with a claim for the entire crop.

Sternaman's claim created confusion for the township board because it was exactly the kind of claim decided by a Justice of the Peace, but Conner couldn't decide it because he was one of the parties in the suit. The township board was a tight-knit group by this time, and Conner, who had been Justice of the Peace on and off now for years, was inextricably a part of that group. The claimant, on the other hand, was an outsider.

Despite the outrageous nature of the claim, the board did its best to treat it fairly. Someone suggested that a constable by the name of Levi Earl should decide the case. Levi Earl, a white man, was chosen possibly on the insistence of Sternaman, perhaps because the board was trying to cover its bases against further litigation in the case.

Once Earl had been selected, a careful record of the entire claim was made by the township clerk in Covert's mortgage record book. This was the only time that such a claim was so recorded, giving an indication of how unusual this case was.

The decision must have been a difficult one for Earl to make, as the crops were not formally divided. Could it have been that the five acres that Conner had planted were flourishing while Sternaman's had not survived the winter? If a wayward wind had blown a portion of snow off the land, drifting it high against the other section, half of the crop would have been lost.

But for all the difficulty and confusion surrounding the case, community ties overrode racial boundaries, and Earl decided in favor of Conner. Sternaman had no choice but to accept the decision.

The township clerk, D. B. Allen, a Civil War veteran like Conner who would soon invite Conner to be one of the founding members of the local Civil War veterans' association, took his responsibilities seriously that day. He used his most formal legal language in the recording of the settlement, as if the formality of the written words would protect his friend's rights. "To wit," he wrote, "the undivided one half interest in ten acres of winter wheat on the premises of Henry Phelps" did legally and rightfully belong to William Conner, plaintiff, for which "I have levied this day a writ of attachment" in his favor.[31] The law came first, not a man's color.

But even while blacks were being treated fairly and equally in Covert, their rights were slowly being taken away in the nation at large. In 1883, the same year that Sternaman tried to take something that rightfully belonged to a black man, the federal Supreme Court stole the civil rights of all black people, reversing the Civil Rights Act of 1875, which had made racial discrimination in public transport illegal.[32] This meant that when Conner visited Chicago on a ferry, he could legally be placed anywhere the white captain decided was appropriate, even if that meant he had to ride on deck, in the teeth of the wind. People of African descent could now be legally barred from entering any public space where whites gathered, from restaurants to barbershops.[33] In Chicago some Justices of the Peace were refusing to allow African Americans into their courtrooms in any capacity but that of defendant.[34] And that was just the beginning.

William Conner and the other people of African descent in Covert would have known that the winds were changing. They were, along with the other Civil War veterans in Covert, getting older, and age did not work kindly on men who had often fought terrible illness, as well as battles, during the war. They must have looked at their children, now reaching adulthood, and wondered if their triumphs would be replicated in the next generation or if the winds would turn completely and sweep away all the changes they had fought for and all the causes they had won.

Chapter 7

Friendship: 1885–1889

If on the ocean sailing,
Or where ere you may be,
When you twine your wreath of roses,
Fasten in a bud for me.

— Written by Emmaline Seaton
to her friend Gertrude Enslow,
January 25, 1889[1]

In 1888 a successful real estate investor in Chicago sat down
at a local restaurant and ordered a meal and a cup of coffee.
Because he happened to be black, the owner of the establish-
ment, not having the courage to refuse him service, instead
charged the black businessman prices ten times higher than he
had posted in an effort to make him leave. The black businessman refused to go, even though he had to pay an outrageous sum for his simple meal.[2] As Benjamin Arnett, a state
representative in Ohio, had reminded his fellow politicians in
1886, "It matters not what may be the standing or intelligence
of a colored man or woman, they have to submit to the
wicked [Jim Crow] laws and the more wicked prejudice of

the people. It is not confined to either North or South. It is felt in this state."[3]

Twenty good years had passed from the time Covert had first been integrated. The young pioneers who had come with their babies were now old farmers with grown children. If the men ever caught their reflection in watering troughs, did they lean back in surprise? Yet these were the faces their wives had hoped to see when the men were gone to war. The women had wanted this age, these years, this rough skin, heavy as old canvas. On both their faces, man and wife, was the record of too many early mornings in midwinter checking on the cattle and too many long days in high summer harvesting hard before the rains came. On their faces also were the heavy grooves worn by tears, like the work of rivers on rock, for almost every one of them from those early years of settlement had lost a child, the cemetery speaking quietly of all those gone. Around their eyes radiated fine lines, like those drawn by children to show the rays of the sun. When they watched for the dust that betokened a carriage full of friends or when they smiled in welcome, the rays grew warmer, more plentiful.

Did the friends, black and white, who had aided and encouraged one another laugh at the differences in aging? Himebrick's face was barely lined, but he and his old neighbor Levi would both have been walking slower and had both been noticing the changes of weather, rubbing their shoulder or knee to ease the stiff soreness there. Their wives must have traded recipes for the best creams to soften cracked fingers, the warmest liniments to bring comfort to aching and tired limbs.

Did their children, now grown, young and supple as their parents had once been, wrinkle their noses at the potent unguents that helped ease their parents' days? They had little need for such things. They were off in a whirl and a dash to gather at church for the young people's meeting, to make it to school before the bell stopped ringing, to hitch up the horses for a nighttime sleigh ride over the rolling hills their parents had transformed from forests to fields.

Based on the number of young people he gathered with, Frank Rood had a life typical of a teenager from a well-to-do business-and-farming family in Covert. He had the kind of face that would have benefited from a beard, but as a young man he didn't wear one. Instead, he wore a mustache whose long drooping ends seemed to point sadly to his lack of chin. At eighteen he was pale and painfully thin, with lovely large eyes and ears that seemed to put the size of his head into an oddly small perspective.

Frank was fun, cheerful, and energetic — and he had prospects. He had almost completed his high-school course work, studying at home with the aid of the local teacher. And he had been accepted into the Michigan State Agricultural College, in Lansing. This meant that, despite the unfortunate mustache, he was quite popular with the local girls, and there were lots of them, for Covert in the late 1880s seemed filled with young people.

These were the second generation, whose parents had managed to survive settling the frontier. How Frank's parents must have lectured him. They had come all the way from Massachusetts to assist their friends and one-time neighbors, the Packards, in their mill work. They had managed to clear land to start a farm, build a house where they could raise their family, and survive a myriad of challenges, and now here was Frank, wanting to gallivant around the countryside with some young lady. Frank's parents, Edward and Flora, may have given up and sent Frank to be lectured by his uncle, David Rood, who lived next door and had recently retired to Covert after living in Africa as a missionary.[4]

Frank did his best. He studied hard and helped with work on the farm, but it is obvious from his diaries that such tasks could not hold his attention for long when there was a young lady to escort. In many ways Frank's life was similar to other young white men's lives on farms in the nineteenth-century Midwest. Reading his diaries, it is almost impossible to tell that his home community was unusual, but Frank took a lot for granted. His schoolmates in his one-room schoolhouse had been black children whose fathers helped govern the township and whose families belonged to his church. None of the radical integration and equality that existed in Covert must have seemed radical to Frank; it was just the way things had been for as long as he could remember.

His weekly calendar was packed with activities, many of them held at the church. There was a young people's Bible study group that met on Sunday evenings, as well as a prayer meeting on Thursdays. Then it was band practice Thursday night (he played the horn) and choir on Friday. Out-of-town speakers often came to the church on Friday nights, and many in the community attended to hear topics ranging from missionary work in Africa to the prohibition of alcohol.[5]

Just as the graveyard was integrated, so was the church. The Conners, Tylers, Pompeys, and numerous other black families were members.[6] There were no pews at the back "reserved" for black members; everyone sat side by side.[7] In Ohio — the state that had once been at the heart of the abolitionist movement in the Midwest — even where churches did allow blacks to attend (which was rare in itself), they most often relegated them to a separate area.[8] But not here.

By 1886 the members of the church decided to make a push to recruit additional members. It being a good Yankee Congregational church, a committee was formed for this purpose. They called themselves the Prudential Committee, and those who volunteered for the job were eight former New Englanders, many from the families who had originally founded the church.

On a cold Sunday evening in February 1886, with church done and Sunday dinner eaten, the minister, John Jeffries, and his wife were joined by Alfred Packard, Horatio Lyon, and Joseph Rood, Frank's other uncle. Their directive was clear. "According to a resolution passed by the church last Thursday," the Prudential Committee was to visit the homes of a number of people each month to invite them to become members. That evening they were starting with eight names; among them were Frank and Emmaline Seaton, the children of Joseph and Nancy, now grown into fine young people.[9] Like Frank Rood, they had probably been attending the many functions the church held for people their age but were not formally members. Although Frank Seaton was nineteen and Emmaline was eighteen, they still lived at home, almost certainly helping to support their mother. There was more than physical support needed, for together they were still grieving for the passing of their father.

Yes, Joseph Seaton was gone, the first black Civil War veteran to die in Covert. Nancy, his wife, and sister to William Frank Conner, must have been barely able to bring herself to think of the reality of his passing. Only a little more than ten years before, her true, rawboned man had been so full of life and dreams that he had taken them all the way to Kansas. By 1885 his laboring lungs could barely carry him through the day. The doctor, noting Joseph's complexion and tainted eyes, pronounced liver failure, but when asked by his good friend the white Abram Brooks "where his misery was," Joseph said in "his side and breast." He did have a hard cough, and everyone had heard it. It had haunted him since the war, and it was now, finally, bringing this "pretty, short, strong man" down.[10] Nancy, hale and strong at forty-one, must have wished she could give Joseph some of her health, her life.

What she could give him was her care — her burden eased by the friends and family coming to offer ministration — and distraction. When the final days came, many gathered round: her family, father, brothers, and children, as well as Joseph's friends. At least two of those good friends were white, the young C. C. Burton, who worked with Joseph at the mill, and Abram Brooks, who had known Joseph for only a few years but cared for him so deeply that when his last hard breath was done, Abram came to help Nancy "lay him out."[11]

Laying out — the difficulty of this task can hardly be imagined today. There is a wreckage of the body upon death that requires hard and intimate labor to mend. On the day of Joseph's death, there must have been a still quietness to the house that he built. And sheltered in that quiet place were Nancy and Abram, bending together over a body, this woman and man, black and white, laboring together, grieving together, bound by love for a man whose body was now past suffering.

Nancy's brother William came to her aid. Joseph had been a proud man, not easily accepting of anyone's assistance. For years his friends, particularly his white coworkers in the mill, had been urging him to apply for a pension. They could see his pain and the way his illness hampered him. They told him many times that the government owed him, but he would not take the government's money. William must have also encouraged him to apply, for he had been receiving a pension for some years now and as Justice of the Peace could have made sure that Joseph's pension did not meet many of the hurdles that most black veterans' pensions did. But Joseph would not be swayed. His early and painful death must have been a bitter blow to his family and friends, for it was confirmation that he had been fighting harder than many knew just to survive the disease that had gripped him since the war. Nancy was now a widow with her four youngest still at home. As soon as Joseph was buried, William put together a pension application for Nancy, and Abram and C. C. gave their depositions before him and a federal agent, their testimonies making clear their warm feelings of admiration for their friend and his family.[12]

By the time a member of the church's Prudential Committee came to the Seaton home to talk with Frank and Emmaline, the siblings would have had a year to grieve, but the pain of their father's passing must have still been a sore burden, and the kind welcome offered by the church must have been a comfort. After that meeting, they agreed to become members, and the other members of the family would soon follow them.[13]

The committee, encouraged by their success, added more people of African descent to their lists of potential members and so began a most extraordinary period in which the committee made it a priority to recruit black members, while other churches, even in the Midwest, were making clear that they saw blacks as second-class citizens.

Possibly at Frank and Emmaline's urgings, the committee turned their focus to the other members of the Seaton family. By April they had asked Joseph Jr. to become a member. Joseph Jr., now twenty-two, had been born while his father was off fighting. Just as he had kept his mother company in his infancy, he continued to live at home now, working at the mill to support the family.

Again a member of the committee visited the Seaton home, this time to talk with Joseph. Joseph must have enjoyed the chat, for he decided to attend the next Prudential Committee meeting, on April 21. Three other prospective members also decided to attend that evening, all of whom were white. After a brief and rather formal introduction on what it would mean to become a member of the church, the group relaxed for the rest of the evening, during which time "every member of the committee and each candidate took part in the conversation that followed." We can only imagine what their conversation covered as this young unmarried black mill worker sat in the formal parlor of the parsonage with his boss, Alfred Packard, alongside the venerable older white women who made up the committee, the young white couple who was considering membership, the minister and his wife, and all the others, enjoying one another's company.[14]

By May 31, 1886, the committee had added Joseph, Frank, and Emmaline Seaton to the membership rolls and now turned its attention to the youngest Seaton child, Ora, only thirteen at the time. At the same meeting they also decided to have the minister visit the Tyler home. Louisa Tyler had long been a member of the church, but Himebrick, despite the fact that his good friend William Frank Conner was a member, had not added his own name to the membership book. George Gayton was also on the committee's to-visit list that night. George and his wife, Martha, were both in their fifties and had recently moved to Covert. They were second-generation black New Yorkers, their families so long in that state that they could have seen slavery still legal there.[15]

Himebrick decided to join, and both he and Louisa (who recently had not been attending church as much as the Reverend John Jeffries would have liked) assured the minister they would attend regularly. John Jeffries was obviously impressed with his visit, for while the committee enthusiastically voted to keep Louisa on the membership rolls, the two white members who had also been lax in their attendance were dropped.[16]

The minister was not as successful with Ora, the youngest member of the Seaton family, and George Gayton. Ora informed the committee that she wanted to wait until her mother became a member, and George Gayton could not make up his mind.

Not to be discouraged, the minister and committee members began to visit the Seaton and Gayton households frequently. By June 29 George Gayton had finally decided to join, and the delighted committee recorded that they "cordially commend[ed] him to the church for fellowship."[17] A month later Ora and Nancy Seaton joined as well. By 1887 three of the Seaton siblings as well as two of William Frank Conner's daughters were meeting weekly with the twenty-eight other members of the Young People's Society for Christian Endeavor (YPSCE) in church members' homes. On the evening of September 28, 1887, everyone met at the home of the Nelson family, local white farmers and neighbors to Himebrick Tyler — a fact that would hold great significance in the future.[18]

A year later William Conner, long a member of the church, must have been grateful for the support of both his church and family, for Elizabeth, his dear Eliza, was gone. Together, in their lonely ways, they had survived the war. He had promised her many things in the letters he had written from the front — a good income, a fine home, and love — and had made good on all of them.

Two years earlier he had aided his sister Nancy in her grief, but now it was she who could aid him. And Himebrick, his good friend, must have been a comfort too — Himebrick, whom William still called brother, even though Himebrick's first wife, William's sister Zylphia, had passed away many years before.

Nancy and William were now widow and widower. As single parents they were rare within the black community of Covert — indeed, there was only one other black single parent in the township, the widowed Abigail Conner, William and Nancy's stepmother.[19]

As death and loss among the pioneer generation became more common, these pioneers became more nostalgic about the past. It had been twenty years since the war's end, and some of the veterans in the township decided that it was finally time for them to start a veterans' organization. So it was that in 1886, the year between Joseph and Elizabeth's deaths, a post of the Grand Army of the Republic (GAR) was formed in Covert.

The GAR was first created soon after the close of the Civil War, in the neighboring state of Illinois. Initially aiming to gather together veterans for comfort and comradeship, it later became a vast organization with clubs that resembled fraternal organizations, with immense political power. By the time the Covert GAR was formed, there were regional and national "Encampments" being held, in which thousands of veterans would come together from the many posts for a gathering that could last many days.

Sadly, by the 1880s it was a sorely segregated organization, with few "posts" combining white and black membership.[20] When the Covert GAR was formed, however, more than a third of the founding members were black, their names as familiar to us now as they must have been to the white veterans in Covert: William Frank Conner, Washington Pompey, Lorenzo Pompey, Himebrick Tyler, and John Conner.[21] William Conner was ranked an officer upon the founding of the post, and as the years passed, at least one African American, although more often two, held a position of officer within the ranks of the GAR, usually within the top three positions of the officers' ranks. All five of the original black members would continue to hold high-ranking positions until their deaths.

Only fourteen men founded the post, even though there were more than fifty Union veterans living in the township.[22] Membership would soon swell as the organization gained popularity. As the Covert GAR grew, so did the power of its black members. Just as the GAR had political clout on the national front, so it could wield real force in the local community, and Covert was no exception.[23] The men who belonged to the club often ran for and won office in the township elections, and their status as veterans was venerated within the community.

One of the first events the men from the Covert GAR attended was the eighth annual Michigan Encampment, in which GAR posts from all over the state gathered in Jackson, Michigan.[24] As the most recent post to be formed in Michigan, Covert's founding members almost certainly met the state commander of Michigan's GAR, the Honorable Charles Long. Like the black veterans of Covert's post, Charles Long had seen fierce action during the war, losing his arm in the battle on Wilmington Island, Georgia. Despite his disability, he had earned a law degree and was at the time a well-respected lawyer in Genesee County, home to the city of Flint, in southeastern Michigan. A year later he would be appointed to the state supreme court, and ten years after the Encampment, the

Honorable Charles Long, now chief justice, would again cross paths with blacks from Covert, with extraordinary results.[25]

At least some of the posts in attendance in Jackson would have been segregated, a potent reminder to the Covert GAR of the unusual decisions they and their community continued to make. Nevertheless, the shared war memories of the Covert veterans became an important bond that helped them to create a group identity that transgressed the lines of race.[26] The Covert GAR members saw themselves as formative in their nation's history and as honored citizens of the nation they had helped to preserve. Their integrated membership was a constant reminder that their nation had survived because of the efforts of both white and black soldiers.[27]

While their fathers were reforging bonds rooted in a common past, the children of Covert were creating new bonds of friendship that were both a legacy of their parents' work as well as entirely new relationships that would outlast their parents' time on earth. And school was proving to be crucial for the continuation of Covert's culture in the next generation.

While there had been advances made after the Civil War in legalizing integrated education in the Midwest, Jim Crow, the name given to the growing institutionalized segregation that was keeping blacks from many resources, was rising across the United States. In the South two decades of brutal repression of black Southerners had unofficially taken away many citizenship rights. Between 1880 and 1888 the number of registered African American voters actually attempting to vote plummeted. By 1888 only half of those who had braved the polling stations in 1880 were daring to risk their lives to do so. In addition to violence, blacks in many portions of the South who attempted to vote were faced with deliberately difficult bureaucratic hurdles put in place to keep them from exercising their rights.[28]

Not surprisingly the rise of Jim Crow saw a growing white intolerance of integration.[29] Even Oberlin College, in Ohio, that bastion of radical abolitionist activities and integrated education, was experiencing setbacks. As early as 1882 the college started seeing a groundswell of racism from its white students, who were refusing to sit and eat at the same tables as their black classmates.[30] In Covert, however, the culture of integration and equality that the pioneer generation had worked hard to create was being passed on to the next generation.

Today, sociologists and those studying race relations in contemporary public schools recognize the problem of self-segregation, in which African American and white students may sit next to one another in class but almost never do so in the cafeteria.[31] While Covert's schools were one-room schoolhouses, not large conglomerated affairs, the children within them still socialized, and within that context there was still the opportunity to exclude.

While every school district in the township that included black children welcomed them, Ora Seaton's teacher would have been white, just as many of her classmates were. (For a chart on African-American school-age children, see Appendix page 225.) Indeed, despite the unusual nature of education in Covert, Covert's teachers seemed to have followed a traditional pattern for small rural Midwestern communities. Covert's teachers were usually young and female. The township school board kept records of every teacher they certified, and none were black. However, they also kept a record of those who applied for and were denied certification, and this record indicates that no African Americans applied for teaching jobs. These white teachers, however, were being approved and overseen by a black man: by 1886 William Frank Conner had held a position on the school board and would be continually reelected to that position for years.[32]

By 1888 Ora was fifteen, lovely, and popular. As she walked to school, she would have been surrounded by beauty, for autumn is a glorious season in southwestern Michigan. Once in the classroom she would certainly have lost herself in the pages of books, now old and aging, that gave off a sweet dusty scent, not unlike that of the leaves outside. The books were old because the township could ill afford to duplicate the extravagant purchase it had made thirty years before. The books may have been worn, and unfashionable in their abolitionist integrationist ideals, but they could still engage a child in reading, and more.[33]

By this period many recognized that textbooks could influence the ways that schoolchildren interpreted the cause and effects of the war, and supporters of the Confederate cause made it a priority to reach children in this way. The war had been won to preserve the union of the United States as a nation and to free her from the bonds of slavery, but the South was attempting to win the culture war. The white Southerner

Thomas Nelson Page began writing immensely popular books during this period that were filled with disturbing stories in which black people were shown as obviously unable to even speak as well as whites, much less be as good. Page's favorite character was the faithful old ex-slave who longed ardently for the good old days of slavery, when he could happily do his master's bidding and be directed what to do, as he was obviously unable to do that service for himself. Jefferson Davis wrote his massive memoir in 1881 entitled *The Rise and Fall of the Confederate Government*. In writing it he gave powerful ammunition that was used frequently in the culture war waged by white racists in the South. Here was the argument that the war was not about slavery and that keeping human beings in bondage had been appropriate because those human beings were of African descent and, hence, inferior and fit only for enslavement.[34] This battle for the hearts and minds of the young was not going unopposed. Northern publishers put out textbooks that were deeply sympathetic to the Union cause, and when the Covert school administrators did buy new books, they were careful to choose these ones.[35]

But the war was being lost. Books that trumpeted the white supremacist South's "lost-cause" rhetoric were gaining popularity across the nation. Their racist descriptions may well have been convincing to the many white children who grew up across the Midwest in communities that had kept blacks from becoming neighbors through the use of Black Codes and social pressure. These children had no black neighbors or black schoolmates to help them to see the lies being perpetrated in the books they were reading. The white children of Covert did, and their lives were very different because of them.

Despite all the passions raised over the books they should be reading, the children of Covert seemed much more interested in those they themselves were writing — their "autograph books." Many of the girls, and even some boys, owned these popular little albums. They were beautifully bound in shining leather or soft velvet and inside were the blank pages upon which only valued friends and family members were allowed to inscribe their names and pen a pretty poem or silly ditty. (The luckiest owners might have a friend who was even willing to paste a bright sticker on the page.) The albums could be taken to any social situation, from school to visits to cousins' homes in the next county. Treasured, many of these tiny manuscripts still survive more than a century after their pages were filled, and every single one that still exists gives testimony to the close ties between black and white children in Covert.

Around the time that Joseph Seaton lay dying, a white student by the name of Flora Grace Reynolds asked her friend Priscilla Pompey, Dawson Pompey's granddaughter, to sign her book. Flora also asked Frank and Arthur Rice, teenage brothers in her school, to write in it. They both signed in a strong flowing script, "Remember Me."[36] The fact that the Rice brothers were young black men would have been a matter for trouble in many communities outside Covert, but in Covert the fact that they were black probably mattered less to Flora than that they were schoolmates who may have helped her pass a test or two.

Joseph's daughters were also asked to sign friends' books. Ora Seaton and the white Gertie Enslow were fast friends by the time they were in their teens, so of course Gertie asked Ora to sign her book. Ora carefully wrote out a little poem there that almost certainly had the two girls giggling:

> Dear Gertie,
>> When traveling down the stream of life,
>> In your little bark canoe;
>> May you have a pleasant time,
>> With just room enough for two.

Gertie then asked Ora's sister, Emmaline, to pen a little something. She wrote:

> Dear Gertie,
>> If on the ocean sailing,
>> Or where ere you may be,
>> When you twine your wreath of roses,
>> Fasten in a bud for me.[37]

Autograph books were not owned just by whites. At least three survive from black students in Covert, including one from Himebrick Tyler's daughter Arvena. A few years after Ora signed Gertie's book, the young Arvena began to fill hers. One of the first she asked was her younger brother, Sherman, who wrote the rather obtuse little piece: "To know that before us is the prime wisdom." She probably was much more entertained by her friend Guy Ashton's saying, which went,

O! Come to my wedding
No matter how soon
And if we have pudding
Don't swallow the spoon.

Humor seemed to be the theme with all the young men she asked to sign, including one from Orlando Reed, who wrote:

Think of me in the dead of night.
Think of me when the bed bugs bite.

Guy and Orlando, both white teenagers, signed themselves, "Your Friend."

The girls' notes were a little more serious. The white Ada Kenney, whose parents had been pioneer settlers along with the Tylers, wrote,

There is nothing as kingly as kindness
And nothing as royal as mirth.

When it came time for Arvena to ask her friend Lola Morrison to enter something in her book, Lola wrote words neither deep nor frivolous. Instead she simply stated, "Remember me as one of your friends." After she had signed her name she added one last word, "Friendship."[38]

The fact that ties were strong not just among those of the pioneer generation but among their children would be crucial in the coming years. The next decade would plunge the Midwest into the most horrific era of racist violence it had seen since Quantrill's savage raid in Kansas. But while conflicts forty years before over black rights and freedom were often between whites, this new violence was between whites and blacks and made brutally clear that the ideals of the Civil War were all but dead and that a new form of race war was beginning.

Chapter 8

Justice: 1890–1896

"He has written his title to citizenship in his own blood."

— The Reverend John Dungill,
Covert Emancipation festival address,
August 1, 1895[1]

The early 1890s were a terrible time in America. The nation was experiencing a severe economic depression, and racial violence was at its murderous worst. Between 1889 and 1894, more than six hundred black men and women were lynched across the United States.[2] Not a few of those lynchings occurred in the Midwest, in communities that the Conners, Pompeys, or other black families from Covert could have traveled through many a time.[3]

The violence occurred in communities where blacks and whites had lived together for decades. Unlike Covert many of these communities were marred by segregation and racism, and during this period tensions that may have been high for decades exploded. After a lynching in Decatur, Illinois, in 1893 (one of more than twenty that would occur in that state in the next two decades), the blacks living in the community asked the deputy sheriff why he did not act to keep the mob from the man who had been murdered. The deputy asked them in return, "Do you suppose we would shoot good citizens for a worthless nigger?"[4]

In the following years, "good citizens" would take to the streets, time and time again, to maim and murder those of African descent. Covert's residents knew of these horrors. They were well acquainted with the outside world and traveled a great deal for business and pleasure. This knowledge must have given an edge to their awareness of race and their continuing choices that fostered equality. As if in defiance of all that was happening outside Covert, the black and white members of the Covert GAR had continued traveling to the national gatherings of their organization. In 1891 they attended the massive Encampment in Detroit that was celebrating the silver anniversary of the start of the Civil War.[5] There was a special reunion arranged for the veterans of the 102nd USCT, the troop William Frank Conner, his brother John, and Himebrick Tyler had all belonged to. There they would have been able to meet with other black veterans and discuss with them the changes in sentiment toward them and their race.

This trip must have been a success, because another one was arranged for the next Encampment, in Indianapolis, Indiana, in September of 1893. That year saw the beginning of the economic agonies that would wrack the nation throughout the decade. Although its causes were numerous, one of the major triggers was the collapse of a number of major railroad companies. Soon thereafter hundreds of businesses and banks declared bankruptcy. Unemployment was so high it was matched by only the Great Depression of the 1930s. Indiana was not a particularly friendly place for blacks, strangers or known, at any time, good or bad. It was a state that enforced some of the strictest Black Codes in the Midwest and had kept legal restrictions to African American immigration well into the 1880s.[6] This was also the state that would soon see a rebirth of the Ku Klux Klan, which would become as popular in the Midwest as in the South.

The Covert GAR almost certainly traveled together. At a time when travel meant horses, and hotels were most often boarding houses or private homes, their journey south down into the heart of Indiana to the Encampment must have been an interesting one for the integrated group. Once there, however, they could mingle with the almost four hundred thousand members of the GAR gathered and find much good company.[7]

It was while they were gone, however, not during their travels, that trouble arose. Back home Sheridan Tyler, one of Himebrick's sons, was tending the farm. Sheridan was a short well-built young man in his early twenties and extraordinarily handsome. It was warm that September of 1893, and there was much work to do. This was a busy season, with the fruit crops coming in and grain ripe and ready for harvest.

The trouble all started when a German friend came by the farm to visit. While the German was greeting Sheridan and the rest of the family, something spooked his team of horses, and they dashed off with the cart clattering behind them. In their startled state the horses didn't run to the road but instead turned toward the drainage ditch that divided the Tylers' land from the neighboring Nelson farm.[8]

Such ditches were a testy business in Covert. Soil tended to be damp in many areas, and farmers with land needed it drained. But drainage ditches often had to cross over dry fields belonging to their neighbors. In the spring melting snow and rains would invariably cause flooding, and it took an astute and diplomatic person to handle the disputes that arose during such times.

The Nelsons and Tylers had been neighbors ever since the Nelsons had arrived from the East, about twelve years previously, and both were well-respected members of the community. Like Himebrick, the Nelsons had a son about the age of Sheridan by the name of John, and he came running out of the house with his brother, Willard, just in time to see the horses make a mad leap across the drainage ditch, tearing the top of the wagon off completely and wreaking havoc on the Nelsons' orchards and fields. The visiting friend and Sheridan had been running as fast as they could to catch the spooked team but were only able to reach it at the same moment John and Willard Nelson did. By that time everyone was out of breath and more than a little overheated.

Sheridan would later recall that John began yelling at him, cursing him "and the whole family, and he said it was a damn nigger trick that the ditch was there." This was a terrible and serious slur in the community. Despite John's behavior, Sheridan tried to remain calm and replied that it wasn't any trick that the drain was there and that they both knew it was to drain the land. As Sheridan summed it up in court, "There were some hot words spoken between us," resulting in the two young neighbors refusing to speak to each other.[9]

When this incident happened, in 1893, Covert's population was the largest it had ever been (more than thirteen hundred), but it was still small enough for word to quickly get out about the fight and of the enmity that now lay between the two men. Family friends may well have tried to patch the rift that had grown between the neighbors, but there was nothing that could be done. Even though the two young men saw each other every day, sharing the same dirt road to get to and from town, they never exchanged a word or greeting and passed each other in silence.[10]

Despite this turn of events and the growing storm of violence that was rising around them, the people of Covert continued in their normal ways.

The Emancipation festivals were still held every August, and the entire community still came out to celebrate. Yet, while race and racism had always been a topic covered by the speakers at these festivals, the advertisements for them only now mentioned race for the first time. In 1895 the Pompey and Tyler families were the ones most involved in the organization of the festival, which that year would include an after-dinner baseball game, a sport that now was popular across the nation. In the advertisement in the local paper, the organizers made sure to stress that "all, big and little, old and young, without regard to race, color, previous condition or nationality are invited."[11]

Nationality and creed had indeed become a pretty big issue in Covert. Swedes had begun to arrive, introducing the children of Covert to new Christmas customs, and a group of German ante-Baptists, who called themselves Dunkards, had also settled and started their own church.[12]

Even through these changes, the schools continued to be integrated. School portraits were now popular, made possible through the technological advance of photography. Everyone had to sit still for a period of time no doubt long and difficult for a youngster. Some of the children in these photographs do indeed look more than a little nervous. This may have been the first time their photograph had ever been taken, and the older children had probably warned them of the large flash that would occur above the man covered in the dark cloth. Despite any worry there is still an easy intimacy obvious between the black and white students. They bump shoulders, lean up against each other, throw their arms out to touch a friend, and lay a hand gently on the overstarched ruffles that flare out from the shoulders of their classmates. Such intimacy had long been the case in Covert's schools, and the photos show that it had continued.

Their parents also continued to forge new bonds. It was not an easy time in Covert, for their economy was making a precarious transition. The woods had all but disappeared into the mills, and by 1889 the logging business had become so unprofitable that Alfred Packard, now the largest shareholder of the mill in Covert, almost went bankrupt and subsequently had a nervous breakdown.[13] But his savior, as well as Covert's, was the soil. The poor sandy soil that was common, and always seemed to be perpetually damp, was ideal for growing fruit. Peaches, cherries, apples, pears, and later blueberries began to blossom in the farms of Covert, buffered from the hardest freezes by the lake, which tempered the weather close to its shores. Ultimately peaches would reign supreme in Covert after the logging boom died.

Instead of pulling apart during this difficult time, as many communities were doing across the Midwest, the people of Covert came together. In the early 1890s eight of the most ardent new fruit farmers in the township started the Covert Pomological Society, which met weekly to discuss new farming techniques. The Packards as well as three wealthy white farmers sat side by side with William Frank Conner, Himebrick Tyler, and Allen Pompey to worry over leaf blights and share information on new strains of peaches they were researching.[14]

By the mid 1890s fruit farming had taken good hold in the township, and its successes were shared by the whole community. Frank Rood, now a sober married man with a degree in agriculture, started a fruit packing and canning business that employed many during the height of the growing season. Packing and preserving work was popular with women, young people, and even old people who wanted to make some extra money, and blacks and whites worked side by side.

Men were not the only ones to reap the top profits. A real challenge of fruit farming is the short duration of the crop. Fruit all across the Midwest would ripen within a month or two of one another, and soon train cars full of delicate ripeness would haul into Chicago, glutting the market. Peaches could be canned, preserving them for both sale and consumption. Apples could be made lucrative if turned into cider. Veteran Washington Pompey was now married to Annis, who was busy raising their nine children. But, in addition, Annis was a businesswoman, owning and managing the only cider mill in Covert. The mill would have been popular come fall, when even the oldest fruit could be crushed and pressed.[15]

Even though there was good money in the fruit business, most farmers knew that they had to stay diversified in their crops. Tender fruit trees were prone to damage from rogue freezes in the spring. Livestock, on the other hand, could withstand the coldest weather safe in their barns. The Pomological Society was only a minor agricultural club compared with Covert's Grange, which was still going strong, with William Frank Conner third in command.[16] In addition to good fellowship, Grangers were concerned with protecting the rights of farmers, and now that Covert's citizens were relying less on lumber and more on farming, the Grange was more popular than ever. And no wonder William Conner was one of the men in charge, for he had always kept to farming; while the Packards were struggling to shift to fruit farming, he was shipping his livestock to Chicago to be sold at a premium in the stockyards there.[17]

While fruit and cattle drove William Conner's success, his friend Himebrick Tyler continued to keep a good flock of sheep. While immune to the frosts that could kill an orchard, sheep were not safe from danger. There were no longer wolves in Covert, but stray dogs were a real problem. A tax on every dog owner in the township raised revenue that was used to pay damages to farmers whose sheep were killed by the animals — a frequent occurrence. When a farmer, justly enraged by his loss, came to the township with a complaint, the township had to decide how much to reimburse him. This was a moment when petty injustices could be inflicted on those who did not meet with the approval of the Justice of the Peace, the official recorder of the complaints. Black farmers across the nation have had a long and bitter history of unfair treatment by government bureaucracy, and the loss of a crop by a black farmer was often cause for double sorrow.

In 1892 Himebrick had been out checking on one of his flocks in a far pasture and found five of his sheep and one lamb killed by dogs. It must have been an ugly sight, for it was late June, and warm. As he approached the carcasses, startled crows and vultures would have hopped away, many too full of carrion to fly. And there would have been flies, which often startled but always stayed.

Keeping in mind the quickness of rot and decay in the summer, he would have soon set off to walk more than a mile to the home of Thomas Randall, the white man who was currently Justice of the Peace, so that Thomas could see that the damage was done by dogs and begin the process of reimbursement. Thomas wrote that he and Himebrick "looked the woods and fields over" to find out if any additional sheep had been killed. They found only a lamb, lame from a bite on its leg, but the rest of the flock was safe. Himebrick told Thomas that he was satisfied that no more sheep had been killed, and two days later, on June 22, he received twenty-five dollars from the township in a transaction recorded by Thomas.[18] Two years later a white farmer whose sheep were killed by dogs was reimbursed at the same rate. Such were the normal routines of life in Covert — occurrences that continued to stand out in stark contrast to life in most rural communities.

While farmers of all sorts were reaping the benefits of living in Covert, the seeds sown by the church and schools in Covert were also gathering a good harvest. Church activities had never been more popular. The church had started Bible study classes, called Sunday School, where like-minded people could gather in one another's homes to read, pray, and talk. Their popularity was such that their membership exceeded the church's. There were fifteen groups made up of nine to twenty-one members, and while many of the groups were separated by gender, none were by race. Seven of the groups had black members, sometimes in such numbers that they accounted for a third of those in attendance.[19] The Prudential Committee must have been delighted, for this was a new way to reach prospective members and expand their roll book.

Frank and Joseph Seaton decided to join the all-male Sunday School Class 12. It was one of the largest, and its members were all respected men of the community. Frank Rood was both a member and the assistant superintendent of the entire Sunday School program, and his father, Edward, was the class teacher. The group was tightly knit, staying together for quite some years. In 1893 they decided to memorialize their good company, traveling to South Haven to a photographer's studio. Joseph Seaton could not make it, but his brother Frank traveled with his friends, all of them in their Sunday best, so that they could gather in front of the camera.[20]

Just as Frank and his Sunday School class had gone to South Haven to preserve their bond for posterity, so too did his sister Ora and her friends. Five of them — Pluma Tacy, Grace Beatie, Jennie Randall, Gertie Enslow, and Ora — had all been members of Sunday School Class 10 for more than five years.[21] They were all long out of school, most of them in their early twenties, but their bonds were obviously close.[22] For their photo the group chose Alice Adams to sit in the center, and she holds a mysterious piece of paper, possibly a letter or their group's motto. Alice, like Ora, was the daughter of a black Civil War veteran, William Adams, who with his wife, Adelia, had moved his family to Covert in the 1880s. Alice's roots were deep in the Midwest, her mother's parents having been born in Ohio. Alice's father had been born in Indiana and raised in a mixed-race family; his father was Scottish, while his mother had been a black woman from Delaware.[23] Despite the fact that the Adamses were not members of the pioneer generation that had settled Covert, as Gertie and Ora were, Alice was still welcomed.

But all was not perfect. John Nelson and Sheridan Tyler were still refusing to speak to each other, even though it had been over a year since the incident of the runaway horses in the orchard. On November 7, 1894, Sheridan got up before dawn and, with his friend John McCreary's help, hitched his mare to his father's wagon to take a load of wheat to the mill in town. Sheridan was proud of the mare, his first horse. She was five years old, strong and thick of girth. Together the two young men hefted the wheat into the wagon and set off. By eight-thirty they had finished their work and started the return journey home. They were still one of the first teams out that morning, and their wagon wheels cut neat grooves through the thin layer of snow. In our time, the road they traveled that day would be considered little more than a track. It was narrow, with just enough width for a single wagon. A little way out from town, they saw Rob Ballou coming toward them in his carriage, and behind him John Nelson, taking his younger siblings, Willard and Sylvia, to school. There were wide, shallow ditches on either side of the road, so getting off to the side was difficult, but Sheridan managed to pull over partially into the ditch so Rob could pass.

The unofficial rules of the road at that time may have indicated that after Sheridan Tyler had moved over for an oncoming vehicle, he could then expect to have the following vehicle pull aside to let him pass. Sheridan pulled back onto the road as John came toward him on the track. They were now coming toward each other along the narrow path, though at this point there was enough room for each to pass, as long as both stayed close to their side of the track.

Then John Nelson did an unaccountable thing. Just before the two carts passed each other, John turned his horse "across the road," forcing Sheridan to move into the ditch or risk collision. Sheridan later recalled, "We was so close together I thought there wasn't much chance to pull the other way or we would have went together. I thought by giving him the road and getting into the ditch he would turn up into the east track if he was bound to go there and be alright and he would not hit me if he turned in the track because I was so far in the ditch." But apparently John had no intention of passing peacefully, and he kept turning his horse into Sheridan. Sheridan's mare, by now turned hard sideways in order to get into the ditch, was broadsided by John's wagon. They came together with such force that the shafts supporting John's carriage rammed into Sheridan's mare and then lifted her entire front end into the air. It must have been a terrible moment, not a single person speaking, just the gasps of the horses steaming in the cold morning air.

Nelson backed his carriage up without speaking, releasing Sheridan's mare. Sheridan, also silent, refused to stop for any further violence that John may have had in mind and left as quickly as he could, steering well clear of the road — and John — for quite a way. His horse limped the whole way home and was in obvious distress. As soon as he got her in the yard, he unhooked the wagon, but she couldn't even make it into the barn before she collapsed and, after no little suffering, died.

Sheridan must have been beyond furious, and, wisely, he decided not to go immediately next door to see John. Instead, he saddled one of Himebrick's horses and rode into town to fetch his friends, who happened to be white. Later they are referred to in the court documents as Mr. Morgan and his son Thomas. He must have valued their opinion on horses and wanted them to come back to the farm to look at his mare. They came straightaway and proceeded to make a close inspection of the body, where they found the spot that John's carriage had damaged the horse's side. Although the skin was not broken, it was recessed like a sinkhole; the wound underneath was large enough that Mr. Morgan could fit three fingers deep into it.

Soon more friends started gathering at the Tylers' farm, including a man later called to the witness stand and referred to as Mr. Jones. As they were crouched over the carcass, John Nelson drove by, on his way into town to pick up his brother and sister from school. Sheridan stood up and yelled over to John, "John, I would like to talk with you." John replied, "I don't want nothing to do with you." Jones then approached John and said, "John, he wants to talk with you; he don't mean any harm; we don't want to quarrel with you." Sheridan interrupted him, finally giving vent to his feeling. "John," he announced, "when you run into my horse this morning you killed her; she died about three hours after that." John angrily defended himself, saying, "I didn't run into your horse, you run into me." Sheridan tried reasoning with him, asking, "Did I cross through there in any way? . . . Wasn't I in that extreme east track and wasn't bothering you and I didn't drive one foot towards you?" John replied that Sheridan shouldn't have been on that side of the road, that it was his "track." That made no sense to Sheridan, since it was John's coming on that had killed Sheridan's horse, so he promptly asked why John hadn't moved over. John gave a rather confused answer, charging that Sheridan had no business being "on that side of the road anyway." As Sheridan would later recall, "That was about all I could get out of him, and I left him." And then he sued him.

In most communities in the country, as far as the law was concerned, a young landless black man had no business bringing a suit against the son of a respectable white farmer; but this was Covert. There may have been some attempt by the parents of the young neighbors to reach some settlement, but in the end the Justice of the Peace had to be called in to arbitrate. The Justice of the Peace at that time was the white William Traphagen, and after hearing Sheridan's complaint, he formally summoned John Nelson to appear before him at the town hall on November 16, about a week after the collision had occurred. John explained to Justice Traphagen that it was not he who had turned his cart, but Sheridan, and the collision was Sheridan's fault, for there was no way John could slow down in time to avoid hitting the horse. The Justice of the Peace must have talked to the others involved, John's brother and sister, as well as the friends who had gathered to look at the horse after the accident. After some time and deliberation, he made a judgment in Sheridan's favor, awarding him the full amount he had asked for: one hundred dollars.

Unfortunately, just like that day on the road, John Nelson would not back down. With his father's support he appealed the case to the next level, where a judge would hear it, and hired himself a lawyer. The stakes had just been raised.

The lawyer they hired was the twenty-eight-year-old Thomas Cavanaugh, who just happened to be an ardent Democrat who had represented his county at the most recent Democratic Convention. Covert was still firmly a Republican town, so the Nelsons' choice of representation would have been duly noted by the community.[24] Democrats were still known as the party of the South and the party of segregation.

The Nelsons had not shown by their actions in the past that they were racist, and they had happily hosted integrated church groups in their home. But the feud between the two families was gaining heat. Himebrick hired a lawyer to represent his son, choosing Alonzo H. Chandler, from the nearby town of Hartford. Little did they know they would be working with him for the next two years.

The Nelsons' lawyer appealed the initial decision, and later that winter the case was heard by a local judge. Despite Thomas Cavanaugh's best efforts, the judge decided in favor of Sheridan Tyler. Furious, the Nelsons refused to pay anything to Sheridan and appealed the decision to the county level. Tired of individual judges sitting alone in a small room, they wanted a jury, hopefully made up of white men, with witnesses called, with deliberations, and with great expense.

Maybe the Nelsons thought the extraordinary cost and trouble of a county court hearing would persuade Sheridan to drop his suit against them, but Sheridan was not giving way. On April 18, 1895, the Tyler family entered the county courthouse in Paw Paw, Michigan. It seemed a small building from the front, but once inside it was grand, with not one but two staircases rising up from the lobby, connecting to two separate courtroom entrances. The courtroom itself, though not terribly large, was a glut of glass. There were huge windows lining the walls to the left and right, and against the back wall was the largest of the multipaned windows, arched across the top and glowing above the judge's bench. The Honorable George M. Buck was presiding, and though he may have been sitting at a good height, the ceilings still soared above him. Then there was the jury. There is no way of knowing what their racial makeup was, but in all likelihood whites were the majority, just as they were in the county population.

There were a number of people in attendance from Covert, both white and black. Round-trip the journey was twenty-five miles along rough trails and dirt roads, long enough to require all the witnesses to spend a night and two days in Paw Paw. The time of the trial was also difficult, for April was when farmers were busy sowing crops, which made even greater the sacrifices of time by the witnesses and friends.

The case must have been close to pulling the community apart. People were being asked to testify for or against friends and neighbors, for or against the young men they had seen grow up, for or against the families they worshiped with in church, for or against the men they did business with on a daily basis.

Sheridan, aided by his lawyer, had taken advantage of this new trial to add to his suit against John Nelson personal charges above the value of the mare. The judge, however, made it clear in his statement to the jury that they were not there to award damages to Sheridan if the horse's death had been caused by some roadway confusion; the only way that Sheridan could receive the award he sought was if the jury decided that Sheridan's horse had been killed because of the "grossly negligent, wanton and willful conduct of the defendant."[25]

Sheridan Tyler testified first, giving an eloquent account of what had occurred. When it came time to tell of John's refusal to speak to him, John's lawyer rose up to object. Thomas Cavanaugh was obviously worried that if the story of the altercation in the orchard came out, the jury might believe that John's actions toward Sheridan were willful and aimed to distress or even damage. The judge struck down the objection, and Sheridan continued. Sheridan's lawyer then asked him how long Sheridan had known John, following with the loaded question, "Prior to the seventh of November what was the habit of the defendant towards you and in treating you?"

This was too much for John's lawyer, Thomas, who leapt to his feet, his voice almost certainly raised as he objected that the question was "incompetent, immaterial, and irrelevant."[26]

The judge stopped Sheridan to talk with the two lawyers, telling them that he was inclined to agree with Thomas, as the question seemed overly general. After deliberating, he decided to let Sheridan continue, cautioning his lawyer that Sheridan should speak only of specific occasions that may have influenced John's actions that day. Sheridan was free to tell the bitter story of their disagreement, including the cursing and racial slur that had been used.

This must have been painful testimony for many of the Covert residents present. The use of such racist language was rare in the community, and it had obviously burned in Sheridan's memory so that he separated it from all the other slights that had been exchanged that day.[27]

Once he was finished, other witnesses were called to testify about the value of the horse and the conditions of the road that day. Finally, Sheridan's friend John McCreary, who had ridden with him in the wagon that day, was sworn in. His testimony corroborated Sheridan's account.

The trial moved to the defendant. John Nelson took the stand, reiterating that the accident had been Sheridan's fault. Various witnesses testified to the validity of his statement, including John's brother and sister, whom he had been taking to school that November morning.

Before the jury left to make their decision, John's lawyer, Thomas Cavanaugh, requested that he be allowed to charge the jury with what he saw as their responsibilities. He was denied. Instead, Judge Buck turned to the jury and evenly summed up the testimony of both the defendant and the plaintiff. He also reminded the jury of the laws of the road but noted that "even if Tyler had not turned to the right, but instead had turned to the left," as long as his actions were done for "prudence and safety's sake," his "action could be considered legal and right." This particular note must have rankled Thomas, for it attacked the very heart of his argument. If John Nelson proved "grossly negligent," Judge Buck explained, the jury had to realize that they were implying that John had a "wanton or willful disregard for the plaintiff's rights." In other words if the jury decided in favor of this young black man, they were casting a serious slur on the behavior and character of a white man. Thomas must have breathed a sigh of relief at the judge's words, but the judge was not finished yet. He ended by stating very clearly that even if John Nelson was correct that Sheridan Tyler was careless in his driving, that fact should not influence the jury's decision as to whether John had deliberately acted in a way that was reckless in order to harm Sheridan.[28]

Based on the judge's words to the jury, Thomas would have had little reason for confidence and calm, but he might have still believed that his client was safe in the jury's hands, for he may well have held the belief that the superiority of race was clearly in his client's favor.

The jury left to deliberate. The twelve men had quite a quandary on their hands. This was a classic case of one man's word against the other's, with the various witnesses obviously siding with their friend or family member. The twist was that one of the men was black, and the jury had to decide if a black man's word was as good as a white man's. This was 1895, when the highest men of science were claiming that people of African descent were fundamentally flawed, from their intelligence to their physical construction, and not worthy or able to have equality with those whose ancestors came from Europe.[29]

After some time the jury returned, verdict in hand: "Gross negligence, in favor of Tyler." Immediately Thomas was up and roaring at the judge, or as the court recorder calmly put it, "The counsel for the defense responded strongly to this judgment." He notified the court that the Nelsons refused to pay what they owed Sheridan Tyler, which was now quite a lot: with the addition of personal damages and court costs, they now owed Sheridan $250.

The Nelsons were determined to fight this to the bitter end, which meant the state supreme court. Thomas Cavanaugh must have been delighted by the Nelsons' choice to continue — rare was the chance for a young small-town lawyer to be heard by such an illustrious court.

Getting the supreme court to hear their appeal took an enormous amount of time and labor, so that spring of 1895 passed and summer came on with no resolution. In August, although still embroiled in the case with the Nelsons, Himebrick and his family worked with the numerous Pompey families to put together a big Emancipation celebration in Covert's Douglass Park, the small piece of green on the edge of town named in honor of Frederick Douglass. The Tyler and Pompey families paid for refreshments, a serious undertaking given that the previous year's festivities had attracted more than three hundred people.[30] Although the troubles with the Nelsons were a bother, obviously they were not endangering the Tylers' financial stability.

The organizers invited the Reverend John Dungill, from South Haven, to give the keynote address. Dungill had given the eulogy at the funeral of Elizabeth Conner's father, Henry Shepard, and was now making a name for himself on the Emancipation celebration circuit. Back in 1891 he had been asked to address the Emancipation festival in Dowagiac, Michigan, where the keynote speaker had been the Honorable John M. Langston. Langston, now in his sixties, was a powerhouse. Although the son of a slave, he had made it to Ohio before the war and there attended Oberlin College, where he earned a number of degrees and soon became an attorney. He had been influential in the creation of the Republican Party, and like many blacks in Covert, he achieved a position in his Ohio township, although his was won in 1855. Soon after the Civil War, he would become one of the first black men to practice before the Supreme Court, while also being inspector general of the Freedmen's Bureau, a federal organization designed to assist the millions of newly freed slaves in the South. He was soon asked to become dean of the nation's first black law school at Howard University. By the late 1880s, however, he was becoming disenchanted with the party he had helped to form. Republicans were beginning to turn their backs on the rights of people of African descent, so when Langston ran for

Congress in Virginia in 1888, he ran as an Independent. He won, but he had to defend his win in the courts for two years before he was allowed to take his seat.[31]

Dungill may well have been inspired by the speech he heard Langston give, for Dungill gave a mighty one in Covert. It impressed the local reporter in attendance so much that he asked Dungill for a copy of the speech and reproduced it in the *South Haven Sentinel*.[32] His speech was, as always, given before an integrated audience, for Emancipation Day was still one of the major holidays in Covert. Dungill addressed them, saying, "To everyone who loves his country, believes in liberty, and equality of right before the law, emancipation day should be the most important of all holidays." He then gave thanks to all those, white and black, who had given their lives to bring an end to slavery, as well as to the families who had lost "sons, husbands, fathers, and brothers" to the cause. He was quick to point out, however, that the freeing of the slaves was not accomplished by white paternalism but that people of African descent had held a crucial role in emancipation, stating,

> God has willed that the Negro should be instrumental in striking the shackles from his own limbs, so when the call for colored volunteers was made the free colored men in the North, and the dusky forms bending over the cotton and the cane in the South, leaped to the front with such alacrity that they dazzled their friends and electrified the world, they as brave as the bravest. The Negro is proud of the fact that he has written his title to citizenship in his own blood.[33]

Dungill then made clear that he was well aware of the rising tide of racism that was enveloping his nation:

> As marked as our progress has been and as great as have been our achievements in the past, we must remember that a nation can no more rely on its past record than an individual. I believe we are just now passing through the most difficult, as well as the most important period of our national development. . . . There are ideas that are wrong, wrong in theory, wrong in practice. . . . slavery in its old form is dead, but the old spirit of slavery still lives. The stripes upon our national banner differ in color as do the races in this country, but they are equal in length and exact in width, which ought to mean in this country, equal rights, equal opportunity, and equal protection for all, regardless of race, color, or previous condition.[34]

Dungill knew of the moves both federal and local to strip blacks of their rights, and as he ended he must have become passionate, his voice rising, the words practically rising off the now-old pages of print, where they are still preserved: "The most important question before the American people today is not of finance, tariff, or reciprocity, but of equity and justice. Shall we have a government of all the people, by the people, and for all the people, or shall we be subjugated and controlled by the slave-holding sentiments of the South, as we were before the War?"[35]

As Dungill stood in front of the crowd, he would have seen the faces of Himebrick Tyler, the Pompey brothers, William

Frank Conner, and almost certainly the gathered members of the Covert GAR, including the white men who had fought for a common cause, to save the nation and free all her people. Looking at these people Dungill asked,

> Let me ask you soldier boys — you who stood between your homes and danger, who have seen your comrades falling upon the right and upon the left, who have looked upon the walking specters of rebel prisons, you who have crossed the bloody chasm of war — tell me, shall the men who tried to assassinate the nation accomplish by bogus legislation, fraud, and deception, what they failed to accomplish with the musket?[36]

To his question, those old soldiers must have answered, whether aloud or in their hearts, "Never!"

And the Tyler family? Dungill's speech must have doubly strengthened their resolve to gain justice in their claim against the Nelsons. That spring they had come close to closure, but by the fall the state supreme court had agreed to hear the Nelsons' appeal.

The Nelsons' lawyer argued for an appeal based on Judge Buck's overruling his objections to Sheridan's mention of "his past relationship with Nelson" as well as the conversation had between the two young men after the accident. Thomas Cavanaugh charged that there had been "'manifest error' of the proceedings based upon those facts and others."

Finally the reply came back from Lansing that Thomas was to have his day in the most powerful court in the state.[37] This time, however, there would be neither defendant nor plaintiff, just Thomas Cavanaugh and Alonzo Chandler, two white lawyers in front of a panel of white judges.

There was a flurry of activity as documents were gathered from all the previous hearings and trials of the case. They were carefully delivered to the justices in Lansing, who would read them over and, after hearing statements from the two lawyers, make their judgment. The date was set — January 14, 1896, a brutal time of year in Michigan, where it if wasn't thawing and mucky, it was snowy and storming. The lawyers had to travel more than 120 miles to get to the state capital, all paid for by the two parties involved.

All the justices read the brief and heard the arguments, but it was the chief justice to whom our attention must turn. His name would have been familiar to Sheridan's father, Himebrick Tyler, as well as to the other veterans who had founded Covert's GAR, for it was the Honorable Charles Long, who had directed the Michigan Encampment they had attended ten years before. Despite his injuries from the war, which besides the loss of his arm included a bullet still lodged in his hip, Long had managed to survive to his fifty-fifth year and was now chief justice of the state supreme court. By January of 1896 he had served as a justice on the state supreme court for nine years and had just been honored with the post of chief justice. *Nelson v. Tyler* would have been one of the first cases he presided over in his new role.[38] Sheridan Tyler could have no way of knowing, that April day in the Paw Paw courthouse, that his mention of his father's attendance at the GAR reunion in Indiana might sway a supreme court justice who was still an active member of the organization. Nor could Thomas Cavanaugh, the ardent Democrat, know that a passionate Republican would be taking over as chief justice.

The judges noted that the case was a difficult one because the testimony "was very conflicting. If the jury accepted the version given by the plaintiff and his witnesses, it is difficult to see how they could have avoided giving the plaintiff a verdict. On the other hand, if the jury had found the account of the transaction to be as claimed by the defendant and his witnesses, their verdict must have been for the defendant."[39] They then spent some time on Thomas's many complaints. Thomas's appeal was based on the claim that there was no motive to what was clearly an accident and that any admission of information about the past relationship between Sheridan and John sullied the case. The justices disagreed, and strongly: "We think this evidence was admissible as bearing upon the claim of the defendant that the plaintiff was wholly at fault as well as on his credibility and the good faith of his claim." Furthermore, the justices, disturbed by the silence that reigned both during and after the collision on the road, noted that the "defendant [John Nelson] says at page 11 of the record, 'My horse came up broadside. I backed out and went on.' Not a word appears to have been said by way of apology by defendant or inquiry made as to whether any damage was done. This also shows the defendant's bad feelings in the matter and his utter indifference as to consequences."[40]

By this time Tyler's lawyer, Alonzo Chandler, must have realized that this, too, would be a clear victory, but it still must have been quite satisfying to hear the pronouncement read and learn that the evidence that Thomas Cavanaugh had objected to so strongly was "admissible as bearing on the question of damages" and "it was also admissible as bearing on the question of motive." Finally, it was all over, the last words on the now-old pages of the court documents reading, "The judgment is affirmed, with costs. The other Justices concurred."

These are dull words, and dry, for such an extraordinary judgment. It was one thing for Sheridan Tyler to expect fair and equal treatment when making a complaint to his own township's Justice of the Peace, but it was quite another matter when the complaint was sent outside the community. In truth, it was a terrible risk, making what happened in Lansing all the more astounding — that a powerful group of old white men sat in an imposing courthouse and decided in favor of a young black man.

Back in Covert the census, taken four years later, in 1900, shows no record of the Nelsons. After more than a decade in the community, the Nelsons had left.

Unfortunately, not all powerful white judges were even-minded. This was 1896, and 1896 was the year that *Plessy v. Ferguson* was decided, making segregation not only official but enforceable. The U.S. Supreme Court, in Washington, DC, made clear its belief in the good of "separate but equal," a doctrine that would be used to rob American citizens of rights if those citizens had even a trace of African blood in their veins.

While much of what the people of Covert had struggled for was being dismissed and destroyed across the nation, in their own community their culture of equality was embraced by their children and by those who were choosing to settle there. Teachers continued to stand in front of integrated classrooms, and the church continued with its popular Sunday School. Every week blacks and whites in Covert broke bread and shared couches in one another's parlors, even as Jim Crow insisted that blacks and whites could not share seating on a public train.

Although it had been a year before the *Plessy v. Ferguson* decision was made, Dungill's Emancipation celebration speech recognized the many challenges the young people of Covert would face in a nation that was turning hostile to their integrated way of life. Some would stay in Covert, while others would move to the cities, where many of their generation were being drawn. Those young people would have to carry on the culture of integration and equality that their parents had created, even as racism gained a strength their parents would have grieved to see. Even though Dungill specifically tailored the speech to people of African descent, his charge was one that applied to the entire new generation in Covert:

> You are to be the fathers and mothers of our future citizenship. Whatever we shall be in the years to come lies very largely with you; therefore be as splendid as it is possible to be. Be grand, grand in your manhood and womanhood. . . . And the day will come when all, regardless of race, color, or previous condition will hand in hand tread the peaceful heights of perfect liberty.[41]

Epilogue

"Ordinary people who learn to believe in themselves are capable of extraordinary acts, or better, of acts that seem extraordinary to us precisely because we have such an impoverished sense of the capabilities of ordinary people."

—Charles M. Payne,
I've Got the Light of Freedom[1]

For a while Covert continued to flourish as it reached its apex in size and success. By 1904 more than 1,800 people were living in Covert, 133 of them black. (For a chart on the population in Covert, see Appendix page 226.) The general population's numbers were swelled each summer by visitors from Chicago and other urban areas across the country who were building "cottages" along the lakeshore, where once there had been a thriving lumber industry. These summer resorts separated themselves from Covert, naming their communities Linden Hills and Palisades Park. Still, the residents relied on Covert's resources for supplies and food, so they would have been well aware of its integrated and unusual nature.[2]

While the summer visitors may have thought of Covert as a backwater, its residents were, in reality, well connected and well traveled. Ora Seaton's uncle, William Frank Conner, was now the deputy grand master of the "colored Masons of Michigan," and in 1898 he attended the national convention of his order in Columbus, Ohio, where Ohio's governor gave the welcoming address.[3] The South Haven paper reported his trip, delightedly informing their readers that "this is an event of national importance to the fraternity of colored masons and confers no little honor upon the men who are to look after Masonic affairs for this state."[4]

Meanwhile, business was booming in Covert, and that business continued to be integrated. There were a number of black businessmen, including Eugene Phillips, who was a carpenter, Sylvester Pompey, who dealt in loans and real estate, and Stephen Gowens Jr., who proudly listed himself in the local business directory as a musician. Alva Adams and Peter Jones were barbers. Allen Pompey, Dawson Pompey's nephew who had been helped by Ichabod Packard when he had first arrived in Covert in the 1870s, was now the owner of the community's only livery stable. He had also bought some of the best real estate in the town, and by 1912 he had thirty acres of prime real estate in the center of the village.[5]

Allen Pompey was now also one of the organizers of the Emancipation festivals, which continued to be popular. Allen and the other organizers were well aware of the rarity of their freedoms and the struggles that had to be undergone to create them. From the haven of the community they had helped to create, they broadcasted to a wider audience their often radical vision. The speakers they chose to lecture at the festivals made it clear that they knew of and struggled against oppression and racial injustice. At the 1901 Emancipation celebration in Covert, where an estimated twelve to fifteen hundred people gathered, a South Haven paper reported that the Reverend F. G. Herbert spoke of "the dominance and avariciousness of the white man." Herbert talked of the fact that whites "stole this country from the Indians and then stole the black men to till the soil they had taken; they had denied the Negro his rights." But the paper added, "He also spoke of the good and humanity that existed in the white man," something that the organizers may have asked him to do, for this matched more closely their own experience of their integrated community.[6] Far from representing the accepted views of American whites at the end of the century, this was rhetoric that was as radical and stirring as that spoken during the civil rights movement sixty years later.

William Conner ran for and won his highest post ever, that of township treasurer, in 1901 as well. What a bitter blow this must have been to his acquaintance from South Haven, the Reverend John Dungill. Just three years previous Dungill had decided to run for treasurer in South Haven. Not only was it his first time running, but it was the first time any person of African descent had run for office in South Haven. He lost the race to his white opponent 170 to 73.[7]

The harder loss, however, would be of William Conner himself. He, along with many of the Civil War veterans, was dying. Washington Pompey died in 1901, Himebrick Tyler in 1902, and William Conner in 1908. They had lived long good lives, but their deaths must still have been devastating for their families and community.

Their families continued to live in Covert, for this was their home, with old friends nearby. Ora Seaton's mother's generation continued with their friendships, as is evident in a photo taken of a church women's group in the second decade of the twentieth century. Although the photo is unlabeled, it is likely that Louisa Tyler and Nancy Seaton are included in the relaxed outdoor gathering.

And while there was loss, there was also renewed life. Even while black men were being murdered for little more than the suspicion that they had had a relationship with a white woman, Covert sheltered its highest number of interracial couples.

There had always been at least one interracial couple living in Covert, but by 1910 there was a total of seven. Sheridan Tyler, who had won his case in Lansing, had now married a young white woman by the name of Millie. A member of the Pompey family was also married to a white woman. Many of the interracial couples, however, were new in the township, and not all of them were young. George Sherlin, of African descent, and his wife, Louise, of European, were forty-four years old and now happily raising their thirteen-year-old daughter, Irene, in Covert. There were few communities where such couples could escape condemnation and threat, but they found a home in Covert.

Death at a young age was still common, which meant that some of the interracial couples in Covert brought children to their marriage from a family dissolved by a partner's death. There was Harry Maxham, who was a thirty-two-year-old white man now married to the twenty-nine-year-old Jessie, who was of African descent. Together they were raising her two children from a previous marriage. Then there were Thomas and Ellen Calloway, who were busy parents indeed. In addition to the two young children they had had together, they were also caring for the white Ellen's two older children from a previous marriage. In this the Calloways had much in common with Thomas and Jane Walden. While the Waldens were a little older, for Thomas was sixty-nine years old and Jane was forty-two, they too had a blended family, raising Jane's white twelve-year-old son as well as their five-year-old daughter.[8]

Raising a family is a challenging prospect, but these families had faced almost insurmountable odds. Interracial marriage, or "miscegenation," had been illegal in Michigan since 1838, and Indiana and Illinois punished the violators of their miscegenation laws with severe fines and heavy labor. Ohio passed its miscegenation law in 1861, adding penalties in 1877 to judges who married interracial couples.[9] Michigan repealed its miscegenation law in 1883, but many of the interracial couples in Covert had been married before then.[10]

Despite the repeal of laws prohibiting interracial marriages in several Midwestern states, social strictures and condemnation of such relationships made them a rare and often dangerous undertaking, especially as segregation and racism tightened their grip across the nation. In 1884 an African American man was sent to the workhouse in Toledo, Ohio, because he and a white woman had just married.[11] Even in 1910, long married and raising their children, such couples' lives would still be threatened in many communities across the

Midwest. A heartrending reminder of this occurred during the infamous Springfield, Illinois, race war of 1908. Springfield, the state capital, had long had black citizens, but that year a lynch mob thwarted from going after an imprisoned man grew to a monstrous size and turned to easier prey — their neighbors. Over a two-day period the heavily armed mob burned black-owned businesses, lynched a black businessman, and, finally, dragged from his home an eighty-four-year-old black man who had been happily married to his white wife for more than thirty years and lynched him.[12]

This innocent man was a casualty in the race war that was rising across the nation. The violence that had been prevalent among Midwestern whites before the war over the issues of slavery now manifested itself along race lines, for there were precious few whites who were willing to risk their lives for black people's rights.

The bloody list is long: in Evansville, Indiana, in 1903, whites rose up in a riot against their black neighbors, and armed white men went hunting for blacks, with any man of African descent unlucky enough to be seen by them shot; in Springfield, Ohio, in 1904, white citizens went on a rampage, attacking the black region of town, burning buildings and beating its occupants; in Greensburg, Indiana, in 1906, white mobs fueled by what they perceived as some outrage by a black against a white went after the black citizens of the community, destroying their homes, beating their bodies, and successfully chasing many of them permanently from the town; worst of all, in 1921, was Tulsa, Oklahoma, where open warfare lasted for days as entire blocks of the thriving black section of the city were bombed into rubble, and despite the courageous efforts of the black World War I veterans who lived there, hundreds of black citizens were slaughtered.[13] These are just a few of the many acts of violence that occurred — the list goes on, an American epic of guns and ropes.

All of these were towns where blacks had been living and working for decades. These were communities where whites and blacks had fought on the same side of the same war. But the blacks of the Midwest were finding that nothing could save them.

By the 1950s Jim Crow's proponents had all but won, creating the biggest lie about American history and culture: that racism had always been the norm and the accepted habit of whites. Sadly, the Midwest played an important part in the construction of Jim Crow, for the racist whites there had been dealing with a free black population for decades before the Civil War and had segregating and divisive patterns and social systems and laws in place that the South — which in its own perverse way was quite integrated — could borrow, and did.[14]

The belief that the racism of Jim Crow was natural and nonconstructed is still common. Even actively racist white intellectuals of the Jim Crow era are still perceived as innocent bystanders, "going with the flow," as it were, of an overwhelming cultural reality. Yet that "flow" was created by just such intellectuals. Cartoonists, authors, artists, directors, scientists, and historians all began to speak on a similar theme: that people of African descent were not truly human, nor worthy of fair or decent treatment. Hitler understood the power of film to sway a nation, but racists in the United States had grasped this concept many years before. D. W. Griffith's infamous 1915 movie *The Birth of a Nation,* which made heroes of the Ku Klux Klan, had its premier at the White House and inspired the rebirth of the Klan in Georgia, a resurrection so strong that by the 1920s many whites across the Midwest were proud and open members of the organization.

Many times it has been said that those who lose sight of the past are doomed to repeat its mistakes. But it could just as easily be said that those who lose sight of the past are denying themselves its lessons of hope and promise.

Why did Covert happen? Although it may be the first question that comes to mind, it may not be the most powerful one. The question that Covert should raise is, why not?[15] Our puzzlement over Covert reveals a hidden assumption that racism is the norm, that unfairness and injustice are the natural patterns that the nation falls into if given half a chance. That assumption is not surprising, given the horrific and sorrow-filled history of race relations in this country, but Covert reminds us that that terrible history was a choice. That choice may have been made by millions of whites over many decades, but it was a choice, not a given. If the residents of Covert were able to create a vibrant and normal community while being integrated and equal, why couldn't the rest of the nation? That is the question; that is the sorrow.

Although some of the decisions that led to the construction of this unusual community seem large ones — such as Dawson Pompey's decision to become part of the political structure of the township and the white voters' choice to support that decision — most of the decisions were smaller. These small decisions were made on a daily basis: a European immigrant's decision to dig ditches in his district under the leadership of an African American man, a newly arrived African American family's decision to send their children off to the local school attended only by whites, a white teenage girl's decision to ask her African American friend to sign her autograph book, a white mill owner's decision to lend money to a newly arrived African American man who wanted to make Covert his home, and a black farmer's decision to help his European neighbor build his barn.

Covert may have "happened" because it was founded by a group of people who had good intentions and acted on them. Abolitionist Yankees from Massachusetts, free black farmers from North Carolina, German merchants, and black frontiersmen who had been born and raised in the Midwest — maybe it was simply their good intentions, lived out on a daily basis, that made Covert.

As Dungill might have added in his 1895 speech, "Be as splendid as your parents have been." Likely enough those parents would have shrugged off the compliment. Yes, people of African descent in Covert had celebrated their hard-won citizenship by running for office, demanding justice, and celebrating their identities as both black and American, staking their claim as central characters in the story of their community and their nation. And, yes, the white people of Covert had not just tolerated but encouraged those endeavors. If asked directly about the unusual nature of their community, however, in all likelihood they would have looked at the questioner with puzzlement, for what was odd about trying to live successful lives with one's neighbors? What was strange about a community where its residents celebrated and supported one another? They weren't perfect; they disagreed and sometimes even fought. They competed against one another in the realms of business and politics.

So what happened to their parents' small community in the following century? First, it became smaller. By the second decade of the twentieth century, most of the black Civil War veterans who had made Covert their home for so many years had died. Their children were leaving to find work in Chicago and Detroit, as were the children of the white pioneers and Civil War veterans of Covert. Emigration from Covert nearly halved the population between 1904 and 1920.

Not only did the entire population rapidly diminish, the African American population did as well. But this pattern of out-migration from rural communities was the norm for African Americans throughout the Midwest. No matter what one's race, farming is backbreaking and difficult work, and factories in Detroit and Chicago offered good and dependable wages.[16]

Yet Covert continued to have unusual race relations into the twentieth century, for it was still known as a region that welcomed black settlement. Even as the grandchildren of the original pioneers of Covert were leaving for the cities, the children of the "Great Migration" were coming to Covert to find a haven from the racism and segregation blighting the urban North. There were some changes and growing racial tensions within the community, but even in the 1950s, when riots were breaking out in the South over integration, and in the suburbs of Chicago middle-class black families were being attacked, Covert's high-school yearbooks show formal "proms" and informal "sock hops" with white and black teenagers dancing together.

Washington Pompey's granddaughter Violet Jeffries recounted what it was like growing up during this period in Covert. She remembers, "I really don't know because I don't think anyone thought of color. We certainly didn't. We were treated the same. I stayed at their homes, they stayed at my home. We ate at their tables, I ate at their tables, and we just played together. We never really thought of race." When she left, Violet noticed the difference: "When I graduated from high school, I went to Chicago and that's the first time that I realized that I was different, because I went to a restaurant with the people that worked with me and they told me, 'Well I'll bring you back something you want,' you know, and I was wondering why, but it took me a long, long time to realize that I was segregated against." Soon afterward she took a trip to Arkansas with a friend of hers, and, as she put it, "We just completely forgot. I went into this real exclusive store and I was looking around and everybody was looking at me real funny and I was by myself, and when my girlfriend found out what I had done she got real nervous and upset and scared. But I honestly didn't think about that stuff."[17]

Violet Jeffries returned to Covert and lived on the very land her grandfather had settled more than a hundred years before. There continue to be returnings to this day, with the descendants of many of the black Civil War veterans of Covert holding reunions in Covert every year.

Just because Covert is a different community today than it

was in the past does not invalidate what happened in Covert in the nineteenth century. Covert's nineteenth-century residents could not know that their community's culture would be different in the future. They were creating a community of radical equality in the face of many challenges, and their accomplishments are worthy even given the changes that Covert would undergo in the twentieth century.[18] Covert has transformed, but that does not change the fact that during a period in our past when racism was on the rise and segregation was strengthening, Covert offered a kinship stronger than laws, stronger than blood, stronger than color.

In the end the story of Covert is about hope, the hope that its residents had that they could create a community of equality. If they were able to succeed, maybe we can believe that hope can reside in our present, and in our future.

Acknowledgments

The first person who should be thanked is Pearl Sarno, who collected and preserved the history of Covert for more than fifty years. Because of her, trunks filled with township documents were saved from being burned, and the last surviving members of Covert's pioneer generation were interviewed. Without her vast knowledge and extraordinary passion for the history of her community, as well as her unending patience with a young historian's many requests and questions, this book could not have been written. Thanks also to Ernestine Carter Taitt, Violet Jeffries, the Rood family, Herman Packard, and all the keepers of the stories. Thank you for sharing them; I hope this book does them the honor they deserve.

There have been many in the academic community who have helped me along the way. Their wisdom, advice, support, criticism, and encouragement have helped strengthen me and my work. Thanks to William Cohen and Marc Baer, who lit the flame and fueled it. Also to Marilyn Strathern and Anita Herle and all those at the University of Cambridge Department of Social Anthropology who helped me to discover the significance of objects, stories, and people and their connections to one another. To Kathleen Conzen and Stephen Vincent, for their generous sharing of advice and information concerning race relations in the rural Midwest. To John Low, who kindly shared information about his people and gently reminded me that the Pokagons have a right to keep their lives and stories protected and private. To Mark Noll, for helping me to fill in some important gaps in the religion and faith of the nineteenth-century Midwest and for sharing my excitement over the role of Congregationalists in America's past. To James and Lois Horton, among the first to understand what I was trying to say about Covert, your enthusiastic affirmation was invaluable during a difficult time. To James Loewen, for encouraging me at the beginning of this project with the advice that a scholar could and should write a book for a broader audience. To Thomas Holt and Julie Saville, for introducing me to so much. To Judith Hunt, an admirable scholar whose mind and heart are both in the right place and who has often rescued me from my own ignorance of Southern history. To Orville Vernon Burton, who early on guided me in working on Covert's extraordinary history. To David Maas and John Fry, whose kind help and careful readings made this a better book. And to Lillian Hoddeson, for helping me to hear the stories.

To the Pew Younger Scholars Program, in particular, Lucie Marsden and Kurt Berends, for their extraordinary vision and invaluable support. And, of course, to the Younger Scholars themselves. Wherever you are, know I miss you and am grateful for our good fellowship.

To the clergy, staff, and friends at Chicago's Fourth Presbyterian Church, whose encouragement and support was so essential.

The work of a historian can seem lonely, but in reality, it is made possible through the generous support and assistance of many organizations, archives, and individuals. I am grateful to the Alumni Fund of the history department at the University of Illinois for its generous year of support; the Bentley Library at the University of Michigan for its research fellowship; the Baker Business Library at Harvard University; the Federal Regional Archives at Western Michigan University; the Michigan Archives; the State of Michigan Library; the National Archives; the Library of Congress; the Government Documents Library at the University of Illinois; the Regenstein Library at the University of Chicago; the Plainfield, Massachusetts Historical Society; the Van Buren County Historical Society; the South Haven Library; Mike Edge at the Greene County Historical Society; and the Gilder Lehrman Institute's generous support of my work at the Pierpont Morgan Library. Special appreciation goes to the Spencer Foundation, whose small grant program made it possible for me to fully research Covert's educational system, as well as the broader history of integrated education in the nineteenth-century Midwest.

My great gratitude goes to the Newberry Library, which gave me intellectual, emotional, and physical shelter as I wrote this work. In particular, James Grossman, Sara Austin, Toby Higbie, and Jennifer Koslow, whose insight, advice, and friendship were and are invaluable. To all the folks who participated over the years in the Newberry Library's Rural History Seminar, for helping to keep the "rural" flame alive. To the ever-kind staff, who always make me feel like I am coming home when I walk in the door. Of course, undying thanks to the extraordinary librarians, who all too often had to deal with me trying to track down some obscure source while wild-eyed with deadline pressures. And last but not least, the 2003–2004 Newberry Fellows: you were truly collegial colleagues, a rare bunch that I will never forget.

For many years my research turned me into a gypsy. My grateful thanks go to those who were willing to give me shelter during this rambling time, including David and Peggy Bevington, Bill and Elsie Lamb, John and Jo Kleis, John and Marilyn Pelrine, and Ifeanyi and Carol Menkiti.

Agents are now the gatekeepers to the publishing world, and I am incredibly grateful to my agents, Jessica Papin and Michael Bourett of the Dystel and Goderich Literary Management agency, for opening the gates and keeping them open. Thank you for your faith in me and my work and, most of all, for your friendship.

To Geoff Shandler, a good man and a great editor. Thank you for sharing my vision of Covert.

One shouldn't have to thank friends, but they deserve it, for it was they who saw me through all the ups and downs that are included in the writing life. I am truly lucky that their names are too numerous to mention. Thank you, every one of you. And to my dearest friends of all, my sister and brother. Amelia, the true writer, whose eye for the craft made this a much better book. And Jonathan, for his quick mind, warm heart, and patient ear. You are both a blessing.

My husband, Michael, may be penultimate in this list, but he is first in my heart. His affectionate support and unwavering belief in me and my work helped me to see this project through to its completion. What wondrous love is this.

And finally, to the people of Covert, because they lived it.

Appendix

African American Population of Covert, 1860–1920

Year	Black Population	Percentage of Total Population	Total Population
1860	0	0	200
1870	57	8.4	681
1880	101	9.0	1,120
1884	115	9.3	1,236
1894	99	7.4	1,336
1900	130	7.6	1,710
1904	133	7.1	1,885
1910	111	7.5	1,472
1920	50	4.1	1,215

Sources: U.S. Manuscript census schedules, Covert Township, Michigan, 1860–1920; Census and Statistics of the State of Michigan, 1884, vol. 1 (Lansing, MI: Thorp and Godfrey, 1886); Census and Statistics of the State of Michigan, 1894, vol. 1 (Lansing, MI: Robert Smith, 1896).

Appendix

Black and White Farmland Ownership, 1870

	Black	*White*
Total Acres Owned* (percentage of total acres)	609 (2.7%)	4,826 (21.7%)
Average Acres Owned per Owner	67.6	77.8
Average Value per Acre of Land	$35.46	$28.90

*Total Acreage in Township: 22,285

Source: U.S. Products of Agriculture Manuscript census schedules, Van Buren County, Michigan, 1870.

Black and White Farmland Ownership, 1880

	Black	*White*
Total Acres Owned* (percentage of total acres)	705 (3.2%)	10,452 (46.9%)
Average Acres Owned per Owner	70.5	112.3
Average Value per Acre of Land	$47.23	$19.43

*Total Acreage in Township: 22,285

Source: U.S. Products of Agriculture Manuscript census schedules, Van Buren County, Michigan, 1880.

220

African American Landownership in Covert, 1870

Landowner	Total Acres	Cash Value*
John Russel	39	$1,200
Washington Pompey	40	$1,000
Lorenzo Pompey	40	$1,200
Joseph Seaton	40	$1,500
William Bright Conner	40	$2,000
Allen Pompey	50	$1,200
Napoleon Pompey	80	$3,000
W. F. Conner	120	$4,500
Dawson Pompey	160	$6,000
Total of 9 Owners	609	$21,600

*Cash value refers to value of land and buildings on property.

Source: U.S. Products of Agriculture Manuscript census schedules, Covert Township, Michigan, 1870.

African American Landownership in Covert, 1880

Landowner	Total Acres	Cash Value*
M. Jackson	22	$600
John Conner	40	$1,000
William Bright Conner	40	$1,000
Henry Shepard	47	$4,000
Washington Pompey	50	$1,500
Douglas Pompey	62	$1,500
Napoleon Pompey	79	$1,800
Himebrick Tyler	80	$2,000
W. F. Conner	126	$4,000
Dawson Pompey	159	$15,900
Total of 10 Owners	705	$33,300

*Cash value refers to value of land and buildings on property.

Source: U.S. Products of Agriculture Manuscript census schedules, Covert Township, Michigan, 1880.

Political Positions Held by African Americans in Covert, 1868–1901

Year	Position	Name of Holder
1868	Highway Overseer, Dist. 7	Dawson Pompey
1874	Constable (1 of 8) Highway Overseer, Dist. 3	Napoleon Pompey Washington Pompey
1875	Justice of the Peace Highway Overseer, Dist. 3	William F. Conner Dawson Pompey
1876	Highway Overseer, Dist. 7	William F. Conner
1877	Drain Commissioner Highway Overseer, Dist. 2	William F. Conner Napoleon Pompey
1878	Highway Overseer, Dist. 6 Inspector of Election	William F. Conner William F. Conner
1879	Township Board Member (1 of 4) Inspector of Election	William F. Conner William F. Conner
1882	Justice of the Peace	William F. Conner
1883	Justice of the Peace Highway Overseer, Dist. 2	William F. Conner Allen Pompey
1885	Highway Overseer, Dist. 3 Highway Overseer, Dist. 4 Township Board (as J.P.)	Lorenzo Pompey Himebrick Tyler William F. Conner
1886	Highway Overseer Township Board (as J.P.)	Himebrick Tyler William F. Conner

Political Positions Held by African Americans in Covert (*continued*)

Year	Position	Name of Holder
1887	Inspector of Election (1 of 3)	William F. Conner
	Justice of the Peace	William F. Conner
	Highway Inspector, Dist. 2	Allen Pompey
	Highway Overseer, Dist. 4	Himebrick Tyler
	Highway Overseer, Dist. 7	Levi Gowens
1888	Highway Overseer, Dist. 7	Levi Gowens
	Township Board	William F. Conner
1892	School Inspector, Dist. 1	William F. Conner
1901	Treasurer	William F. Conner

Sources: Covert Township Voting Records, 1854–1896 (Covert Museum, Covert, MI); School Census Records, Covert Township (Covert Museum, Covert, MI); Pearl Sarno, *A Look at Covert's Heritage* (South Haven, MI: Sarno, 1994).

African American Population of Covert by School District, 1866–1901

Year	District 1	District 2	District 3	District 4	District 5	District 6
1866	NA	NA	NA	8 (32%)	NA	NA
1872	9 (17%)	NA	NA	6 (17%)	5 (7%)	2 (10%)
1892	9 (17%)	1 (1%)	0 (0%)	0 (0%)	17 (9%)	9 (20%)
1901	10 (19%)	0 (0%)	12 (24%)	0 (0%)	4 (3%)	5 (8%)

Note: Percentages are based only on the particular school district's total population.

Source: School Census Records, Covert, Michigan, 1866–1901 (Covert Museum, Covert, MI). The importance of the school census was not that every single child on it attended school, but that every single child was deliberately counted. Census takers were both black and white, and they went to every home, to count every child in every district, making it clear to parents and to the community that no matter what the race of a child, he or she was a potential "scholar."

The table gives a false tale of segregation, particularly in District 4. The first African Americans to settle in Covert bought some of the best land in the township, close to the center of Covert. While some of it was already cleared, making it ideal for farming, the rest was prime timberland, which they would later sell at a good profit to the lumber mills. These families kept that land throughout the rest of the century, even as their children grew and bought land of their own. This region of the township was School District 4, and the young black families that settled there also sent their children to the school, but by the time the children were past school age, there was little opportunity for anyone, black or white, to buy land in the region and, hence, few children of any race to attend school in District 4.

Total Population of Covert, 1860–1920

Year	Population
1860	200
1870	681
1880	1,120
1884	1,236
1894	1,336
1900	1,710
1904	1,885
1910	1,472
1920	1,215

Sources: U.S. Manuscript census schedules, Covert Township, Michigan, 1860–1920; Census and Statistics of the State of Michigan, 1884, vol. 1 (Lansing, MI: Thorp and Godfrey, 1886); Census and Statistics of the State of Michigan, 1894, vol. 1 (Lansing, MI: Robert Smith, 1896).

Notes

Introduction

1. Wright, *12 Million Black Voices*, 146. My grateful thanks to Cornel West, whose book *Race Matters* first introduced me to Wright's powerful words.

2. Ibid., 43.

3. Turner, "Introduction," 16.

Chapter 1 The Bleeding Heartland

1. The Iowa Quakers Salem Anti-Slavery Society constitution as quoted in Dykstra, *Bright Radical Star*, 30.

2. Larson, "Pigs in Space," 72.

3. Litwack, *North of Slavery*, 3; Painter, *Sojourner Truth*, 20–23.

4. Berlin, *Many Thousands Gone*, 233.

5. Franklin and Moss, *From Slavery to Freedom*, 116–17, 120–21.

6. Ibid., 117.

7. Painter, *Sojourner Truth*, 11–13, 32–33, 35.

8. Franklin and Moss, *From Slavery to Freedom*, 141; Painter, *Sojourner Truth*, 15–17. In her excellent book on the life of Sojourner Truth, Painter examines some of the psychological implications of the physical torture that many slaves endured.

9. Thomas Jefferson as quoted in Adams and Sanders, *Alienable Rights*, 94.

10. Franklin and Moss, *From Slavery to Freedom*, 123.

11. Oberlin Covenant as quoted in Padgett, "Evangelicals Divided," 262.

12. Padgett, "Evangelicals Divided," 262.

13. Ibid.; Litwack, *North of Slavery*, 139; Horton and Horton, *In Hope of Liberty*, 218; Squibb, "Roads to Plessy," 14.

14. Waite, "Segregation of Black Students," 344–64; Padgett, "Evangelicals Divided," 263.

15. While little has been written on black rural settlement in the nineteenth-century Midwest, particularly when compared to the plethora of work on the rural South, there have been some notable books that at least touch on the subject published over the last fifty years. See, for example: Zachary Cooper, *Black Settlers in Rural Wisconsin* (Madison: Wisconsin Historical Society Press, 1977); Nell Painter, *Exodusters* (New York: Knopf, 1977); Jack Salzman, David Lionel Smith, and Cornel West, eds., "Illinois," "Indiana," "Iowa," "Kansas," "Missouri," "Nebraska," "North Dakota," "South Dakota," "Wisconsin" in the *Encyclopedia of African-American Culture and History* (1996); Thornbrough, *The Negro in Indiana;* Vincent, *Southern Seed, Northern Soil;* Walker, *Free Frank;* Gerber, *Black Ohio;* Wilson, *A Rural Black Heritage;* Hesslink, *Black Neighbors;* Dykstra, *Bright Radical Star.*

16. Reynolds, *John Brown: Abolitionist*, 89, 125–32.

17. Franklin and Moss, *From Slavery to Freedom*, 188.

18. Ibid., 123.

19. Ibid., 191.

20. U.S. Manuscript census schedule, Cass County, Cassopolis Township, MI, 1860.

21. Sawyer, "Surviving Freedom," 46, 65. Founded in the 1830s by a group of abolitionist Quakers, Cass County became a major stop on the Underground Railroad before the war. The historian George Hesslink suggests that as many as one out of every four fugitive slaves bound for Canada passed through Cass County between 1830 and 1860. (See Hesslink, *Black Neighbors*, 31, 37.) However, most of the African Americans who actually came from the South to settle in Cass County were not escaping but were free already (Stewart, "Migration of a Free People," 34).

22. Sawyer, "Surviving Freedom," 64–65.

23. Franklin and Moss, *From Slavery to Freedom*, 187.

24. Ibid., 185–86.

25. Ibid., 185–87. A number of different stories and reports exist about John Fairfield and his activities, many of them conflicting in their descriptions of his character, his exploits, and even his death. This is not surprising, as secrecy, misinformation, and subterfuge were essential to the work of any conductor. Almost certainly many other conductors' heroic activities were so well hidden that their stories are forever lost to us.

26. For a fuller discussion of how historians have studied and understood slavery, see Foner, "Slavery, the Civil War, and Reconstruction," and Holt, "African-American History."

27. Dykstra, *Bright Radical Star,* 91–92. Dykstra's book is the source for the John Walker story.

28. Ibid., 93.

29. Ibid., 94.

30. Ibid., 95–97.

31. For more on Elijah Lovejoy, see the Web site for Alton, Illinois, at http://www.altonweb.com/history/lovejoy/.

32. For an excellent and engaging book on the violence at Deerfield, Massachusetts, see John Demos, *The Unredeemed Captive* (New York: Vintage, 1995).

33. Sarno, *Covert's Heritage,* 3, 8.

34. White, *The Middle Ground,* ix–1, 47–48, 50–93, 448–49, 488–93, 523.

35. Ibid., 1–49.

36. Hinderaker, "Liberating Contrivances," 72.

37. Satz, "Indian Policy," 80.

38. Gray, *The Yankee West,* 3–4.

39. Covert Voting Records, Covert Museum, Covert, MI.

40. Kirkland, *A New Home,* 7, 8–9.

41. Berlin, *Many Thousands Gone,* 58–63. Berlin argues that there was a difference between the people of African descent who arrived in the Americas in the seventeenth and early eighteenth centuries and those who were brought over later in much larger numbers to work en masse on large plantations. He calls the

first group the Charter generation. It is very likely that the Conners and the Tylers were descendants of this Charter generation.

42. Franklin and Moss, *From Slavery to Freedom*, 149–50.

43. Berlin, *Many Thousands Gone*, 278.

44. Franklin and Moss, *From Slavery to Freedom*, 156–57. Although a work of fiction, *The Known World*, by Edward P. Jones, is a brilliant and fascinating exploration of what life might have been like for black slave owners.

45. Franklin and Moss, *From Slavery to Freedom*, 146–47.

46. Ibid., 151; Walker, *Free Frank*, 10–12.

47. Franklin and Moss, *From Slavery to Freedom*, 153; Ora Seaton Clark and J. R. Spelman, eds., "The J. R. Spelman Story: A History of Covert, Chapter III," *South Haven Tribune* (South Haven, MI), July 4, 1952.

48. Sawyer, "Surviving Freedom," 24; Berlin, *Slaves without Masters*, 316–17, 334–36; Franklin and Moss, *From Slavery to Freedom*, 154.

49. Vincent, *Southern Seed, Northern Soil*, xii; Cox, "Nineteenth-Century African Americans," n.p.

50. Vincent, *Southern Seed, Northern Soil*, xi.

51. Ibid., 26.

52. Squibb, "Roads to Plessy," 7–13.

53. Dykstra, *Bright Radical Star*, 27.

54. See James Loewen's book *Sundown Towns* (New York: New Press, 2005) for a full and fascinating discussion of the persistence of racism and segregation in the rural and small-town Midwest.

55. Sarno, *Covert's Heritage*, 6; U.S. Manuscript census schedules, Deerfield Township, MI, 1860.

56. U.S. Manuscript census schedules, Deerfield Township, MI, 1860.

57. For a helpful reference to both the first and second Treaties of Chicago, see the Pedia Web site at http://thepedia.com/define/Treaty_of_Chicago.

58. Sawyer, "Surviving Freedom," 135–37.

59. Ibid., 38–40.

60. Satz, "Indian Policy," 80.

61. Tanner, *Great Lakes Indian History*, 96–99, 126, 135, 137; Clifton, *The Pokagons*, xii, 51. Remember, the methods used for counting indigenous peoples, particularly those indigenous peoples who did not want to be counted, were inaccurate, to say the least.

62. Sawyer, "Surviving Freedom," 41.

63. Joseph Toquin, Weso Neota ("Wesaw Mota"), and Aseto Neota all bought forty-acre plots in Covert (then Deerfield) Township from the federal government on July 24, 1854; RG80-116 Tract Books, 1818-1962 (Microfilm roll #6475), State of Michigan Archives, Lansing, MI.

64. "List of the Voters at the Township Meeting," April 2, 1860; "Pool [sic] Book of the Election in the Township of Deerfield," November 6, 1860; both from the Covert Museum, Covert, MI.

65. "Covert Pioneer Sisters," 1937, unpublished document, Covert Museum, Covert, MI, n.p.; Sarno, *Covert's Heritage*, 6.

66. Sarno, *Covert's Heritage*, 6.

67. "Covert Pioneer Sisters," 1937, unpublished document, Covert Museum, Covert, MI, n.p.; Sarno, *Covert's Heritage*, 6.

68. Brown, "Violence," 396–98.

Chapter 2 The Journey: 1860–1866

1. Editorial, *Illinois State Journal* (Springfield), March 22, 1862, as quoted in Voegeli, *Free But Not Equal*, 28.

2. National Archives, pension of Himebrick Tyler, pension of Nancy Seaton, pension of William F. Conner. Unfortunately, as was often the case with black Civil War veterans' pension requests, they were often challenged, and a number of depositions had to be taken proving when and with whom they arrived in Covert. These depositions offer a rich source of information.

3. By 1850, four hundred African Americans *allowed* themselves to be counted in Cass County, although many more lived there and hid themselves from federal or state census men (Sawyer, "Surviving Freedom," 47; Hesslink, *Black Neighbors*, 31, 37).

4. Berwanger, *Frontier Against Slavery*, 32; Berwanger, "Western Anti-Negro Sentiment," 2, 10; Gerber, *Black Ohio*, 9.

5. Obituary for Henry Shepard, *South Haven Sentinel* (South Haven, MI), July 26, 1884.

6. Nathan A. Thomas, notebook, 1874, Arthur Kooker Collection, Bentley Historical Library, University of Michigan, Ann Arbor, MI, n.p.

7. *Times* (Dubuque, IA), December 20, 1862, as quoted in Voegeli, *Free But Not Equal*, 65.

8. Payne, "Whole United States," 89.

9. National Archives, pension of Nancy Seaton.

10. Ora Seaton Clark and J. R. Spelman, eds., "The J. R. Spelman Story: A History of Covert, Chapter III," *South Haven Tribune* (South Haven, MI), July 4, 1952.

11. National Archives, pension of Nancy Seaton.

12. National Archives, pension of Himebrick Tyler; pension of Nancy Seaton; U.S. Bureau of the Census, *Census*, 1860, 8th, 1870, 9th, 1880, 10th, 1900, 12th (Washington, DC: Government Printing Office).

No known images of Conner survive to this day, although he did have some taken, including one of him in his full Civil War regalia that he was particularly proud of. Other records have survived, however, that make it clear that Conner was a man whose African ancestry showed pure and proud. He held a deep pride in the unique heritage his ancestry had brought him, even as he struggled to be free of the racism that often arose in response to it.

13. Heinegg, "Free African Americans," Conner Family (Web page publication: http://www.freeafricanamericans.com/Church_Cotanch.htm); Tyler Family (http://www.freeafricanamericans.com/Tann_Viers.htm). Grateful thanks also to Ernestine Carter Taitt for her extraordinary research into the histories of the Conner and Tyler families.

14. Ora Seaton Clark and J. R. Spelman, eds., "The J. R. Spelman Story: A History of Covert, Chapter III," *South Haven Tribune* (South Haven, MI), July 4, 1952.

15. Ibid.

16. Confederate papers, Greene County, North Carolina, 3rd Regiment, Company A (Greene County Historical Society, Greene County, NC). Thanks go to

Mike Edge at the Greene County Historical Society, who confirmed this information.

17. *Times* (Dubuque, IA), July 12, 1862, as quoted in Voegeli, *Free But Not Equal,* 99.

18. Franklin and Moss, *From Slavery to Freedom,* 217.

19. Sawyer, "Surviving Freedom," 97–98, 103, 117–18.

20. National Archives, pension of William F. Conner.

21. Letter written by William Frank Conner to his wife, Elizabeth A. Conner, November 19, 1864, from the collection of the Covert Museum, Covert, MI; quote from Sergeant James M. Trotter of the Massachusetts 55th included in the Edward W. Kinsley Papers from Duke University as quoted in Trudeau, *Like Men of War,* 326.

22. Soule, *Philadelphia Weekly Times,* May 1, 1884, as quoted in Trudeau, *Like Men of War,* 323.

23. Blight, *Race and Reunion,* 142. It is no secret that General Forrest later went on to help form the Ku Klux Klan and was appointed its first Grand Wizard in 1867.

24. Trudeau, *Like Men of War,* 326; *New York Herald,* December 4, 1864 as quoted in ibid., 328–29.

25. Trudeau, *Like Men of War,* 329.

26. Ibid., 331

27. Dyer, *War of the Rebellion,* 834.

28. South Carolina Department of Archives and History, John Jenkins Papers, as quoted in Trudeau, *Like Men of War,* 330.

29. Robertson, *Michigan in the War,* 490–91.

30. Ibid.

31. Clark and Spelman, eds., "The J. R. Spelman Story"; National Archives, pension of Himebrick Tyler; pension of Nancy Seaton. U.S. Bureau of the Census, *Census,* 1870, 9th (Washington, DC: Government Printing Office).

32. National Archives, pension of Himebrick Tyler.

33. Ibid.

34. Nuclear families were the norm for African American communities in Cass County, as Sawyer, "Surviving Freedom," makes clear in her amazingly lucid and moving thesis on the community (68–71).

35. Letter written by William Frank Conner to his wife, Elizabeth A. Conner, November 19, 1864.

36. National Archives, pension of Himebrick Tyler.

37. "Deerfield Township Report of Taxable Property, 1866," private collection of Pearl Sarno, Covert, MI.

Chapter 3 Rights: 1866–1869

1. National Archives, Washington L. Pompey pension claim.

2. While many scholars have written on the concepts and ideologies surrounding the settling of the Midwestern frontier, two recent books give a broad and fresh overview of the region, for which the author is gratefully indebted. The first is Cayton and Gray, *American Midwest,* a collection of essays; the second, Gjerde, *Minds of the West,* offers insight into the ways in which the Midwest was envisioned and utilized by the various groups settling there in the nineteenth century.

3. Photographic evidence as well as federal census reports make clear that the Tylers were very dark-skinned. The Conners, like the Tylers, were always designated "black" on federal census records, not "mulatto," which was often an option for census takers in the nineteenth century. Descriptions from their military records also make it clear that they were very dark. While no photographs survive of William, Nancy, and John Conner, who came with their families to Covert in the 1860s, photos of their children, such as Nancy's son Frank Seaton and William's daughter Myrtie, make clear that they were not light-skinned like the Pompeys. This is significant, as the Conners and Tylers gained as much power and social standing within Covert as the Pompeys did, if not more.

4. Dykstra, *Bright Radical Star,* 35.

5. Ibid., 92.

6. *Statistics of Michigan,* 689.

7. Voegeli, *Free But Not Equal,* 77–78.

8. Berwanger, *Frontier Against Slavery*, 32; Berwanger, "Western Anti-Negro Sentiment," 1, 90, 109–10.

9. For an excellent overview of the dialogue on race and rights between the two parties in the Midwest during the Civil War, see Voegeli, *Free But Not Equal*.

10. Ibid., 88.

11. National Archives, Washington L. Pompey pension claim; Lorenzo Pompey pension claim.

12. Ada Gowens, interview by Pearl Sarno, 1976, tape recording, Covert Museum, Covert, MI.

13. Violet Jeffries, Verna Curtis, and Faith Fennel, interview by author, September 21, 1996, cassette tape, in author's possession.

14. Obituary for Henry Shepard, *South Haven Sentinel* (South Haven, MI), July 26, 1884.

15. Bates, *History of the Pennsylvania Volunteers*, 968, 971.

16. Voegeli, *Free But Not Equal*, 88.

17. National Archives, Washington L. Pompey pension claim; Lorenzo Pompey pension claim.

18. Lake, *Atlas of Van Buren County;* Ora Seaton Clark and J. R. Spelman, eds., "The J. R. Spelman Story: A History of Covert, Chapter III," *South Haven Tribune* (South Haven, MI), July 4, 1952.

19. Cha-Jua, *America's First Black Town*, 109–12.

20. Vander Velde, "Michigan Supreme Court," 107, 122; Stephenson, *Race Distinctions*, 187.

21. For more on Yankee settlement in this period and the ways in which the settlers carried lifeways with them from the East, see Gray, *Yankee West*.

22. "Annual Report of School Inspectors of the township of Deerfield, County of Van Buren, for the year 1864," from the State of Michigan Archives, Lansing, Michigan.

23. McCaul, *Black Struggle*, 51.

24. The census from 1860 clearly shows that Deerfield, later known as Covert, was a community that had been recently settled by Yankees. Of the adults

twenty-one and over, 56 percent were born in New York, and 56 percent of the adolescents age eleven to twenty were also born in New York. On the other hand, 74 percent of the children ten and under were born in Michigan. It was a young population, with 62 percent younger than twenty years old. (U.S. Manuscript census schedules, Van Buren County, MI, 1860.)

By 1870 the first African American settlers were appearing in the census. They were also made up of young families, and 62 percent of their total population was younger than twenty, just as the white population had been ten years earlier. The African American population twenty-one years and older came from many states, with 28 percent from Indiana, 19 percent from Virginia, and the others from North Carolina, Kentucky, Maryland, Louisiana, and Michigan. Of their children twenty and under, 88 percent were born in Michigan. (U.S. Manuscript census schedules, Van Buren County, MI,1870.) Meanwhile, the white population was aging, with only 52 percent twenty and younger, although they were still primarily from New York.

25. For an excellent and intriguing look at *McGuffey Readers* and their often-abolitionist authors, see "McGuffey and the Abolitionists" in Robinson, *Death of Adam,* 126–49.

26. U.S. Manuscript census schedules, Van Buren County, MI, 1870.

27. Cayton and Onuf, *Midwest and the Nation, 95;* "Annual Report of Van Buren County School Superintendent," *South Haven Sentinel* (South Haven, MI), January 8, 1870, 3.

28. U.S. Manuscript census schedules, Van Buren County, MI, 1870; School Census Record, Deerfield, Michigan, 1866, Covert Museum, Covert, MI.

29 Lake, *Atlas of Van Buren County,* 532–35.

30. National Archives, pension of Himebrick Tyler.

31. In 1870 the highest level of education offered in Covert was eighth grade. In this frontier community, children were needed to help work on the homestead. The reason that such a small percentage of children is shown attending school in Covert in 1870 is because the total number of children recorded reflects the state assumption that all single young people between the ages of five and nineteen were possible scholars, and were counted as such. If only children aged five to twelve are counted in 1870 against those attending school, the percentages change radically, with 66 percent of white children attending and 69 percent of black children attending (U.S. Manuscript census schedules, Van Buren County, MI, 1870).

32. "Annual Report of School Inspectors of the township of Deerfield, County of Van Buren, for the year 1864," from the State of Michigan Archives, Lansing, MI. My grateful thanks go to the Spencer Foundation for giving me the resources to research this and the other extraordinary stories surrounding Covert's integrated educational system.

33. Ibid.

34. The collection had belonged to Lafayette Township, which was cut into three smaller sections in 1856, one of which was Covert (Covert Township Records, 1856, Covert Historical Society, Covert, MI).

35. *Statistics of Michigan,* 689; Carpenter, History of American Schoolbooks, 16–17.

36. U.S. Manuscript census schedule, Van Buren County, MI, 1870.

37. Ballou, *Lady of the West,* 2, 532.

38. Ibid., 532, 542.

39. Ibid.

40. Ibid., 534.

41. Ibid., 524.

42. Hildreth, *White Slave,* 3–4.

43. Hart, "Richard Hildreth," in *Oxford Companion,* 290.

44. Stowe, *Dred,* 18.

45. Ibid., 22. In fact, Stowe includes the "Confessions of Nat Turner" as published in 1831.

46. Ibid., 15–16, 21–22, 672, 679.

47. U.S. Manuscript census schedule, Van Buren County, MI, 1870.

48. Shattuck, "Reminiscence," Covert Museum, 3–5.

49. Ibid.

50. Lake, *Atlas of Van Buren County,* 331; National Archives, Washington L. Pompey pension claim.

51. National Archives, Washington L. Pompey pension claim.

52. Painter, *Sojourner Truth,* 211.

53. U.S. Manuscript census schedule, Whitley County, IN, 1850, 1860.

54. *History of Berrien*, 436; U.S. Products of Agriculture Manuscript census schedules, Covert Township, MI, 1870.

55. Rowland, *Van Buren County*, 476.

56. Zinn, *People's History*, 235.

57. Martin, *Standard of Living*, 412; Long, *Wages and Earnings*, 42.

58. Vander Velde, "Michigan Supreme Court," 112; Jelks, "Race, Respectability," 34–36. As these texts make clear, William Dean ultimately won his case, and the state of Michigan officially allowed men less than one-quarter "black" to vote, but even after this decision was made, Dean's son was turned back at the polls when he tried to vote.

59. Squibb, "Roads to Plessy," 60.

60. "Report of Highway Commissioner's Expenditures, 1868, Covert Township Records; and Highway Overseer Report for Deerfield Township, Van Buren County, Michigan, 20 May 1875," Covert Museum, Covert, MI.

61. Adams and Sanders, *Alienable Rights*, 211.

62. Blight, *Race and Reunion*, 114.

63. Covert Township Records, 1854–1896, Covert Museum, Covert, MI.

64. The fact that African Americans were elected to township positions was not because they were of so little importance that the white electorate did not feel it worth their while to bar people of African descent from running for office. On the contrary, in the rural counties of the Midwest in the nineteenth century, township elections were very important. Township officials were responsible for almost all aspects of the community's infrastructure. Those elected had to oversee the building and running of schools; the funding, building, and upkeep of the roads and railroads; the digging and maintaining of the drainage system; and the policing of the township.

65. Covert Township Records, 1854–1896, Covert Museum, Covert, MI.

66. Chattel mortgage document between Samual Jamison and "Dorson" Pompey, June 21, 1869, private collection of Pearl Sarno, Covert, MI.

67. U.S. Manuscript census schedule, Van Buren County, MI, 1870.

68. Blight, *Race and Reunion*, 120.

Chapter 4 Citizenship: 1870–1875

1. Benjamin Tanner, *Christian Recorder* (Philadelphia, PA), October 3, 1868, as quoted in Blight, *Race and Reunion*, 100.

2. Shattuck, "Reminiscence," Covert Museum, Covert, MI, 3–5.

3. Gertrude Enlow Kenney (age 96), "Butchering Day on a Michigan Farm," August 1972, Covert Museum, Covert, MI.

4. Violet Jeffries, Verna Curtis, and Faith Fennel, interview by author, September 21, 1996, cassette tape, in author's possession.

5. Covert Township Voting Records, 83–85; Rubenstein and Ziewacz, *Michigan*, 108; Squibb, "Roads to Plessy," 57–59; Berwanger, *Frontier Against Slavery*, 40; Thornbrough, *Negro in Indiana*, 250.

6. It was very rare for men of African descent to win this position in nineteenth-century America. See Vincent, *Southern Seed, Northern Soil*, 130.

7. Cha-Jua, *America's First Black Town*, 104.

8. Adams and Sanders, *Alienable Rights*, 221.

9. Advertisement, *South Haven Sentinel* (South Haven, MI), August 24, 1872 (Bentley Historical Library Collection, University of Michigan, Ann Arbor, MI), n.p.

10. U.S. Manuscript census schedule, Van Buren County, MI, 1880.

11. Tiffany, *Treatise on the Powers*, 131, 320, 317.

12. "Mrs. Nancy Seaton Came to This State From No. Carolina," *South Haven Sentinel* (South Haven, MI), 1952; Cohen, *At Freedom's Edge*, 168–74; Bogue, "An Agricultural Empire," 287.

13. National Archives, pension of Nancy Seaton.

14. U.S. Manuscript census schedule, Whitley County, IN, 1850; U.S. Manuscript census schedule, Van Buren County, MI, 1870.

15. U.S. Products of Agriculture Manuscript census schedules, Covert Township, MI, 1870.

16. *Statistics of Michigan*, 689.

17. *Portrait and Biographical Record*, 535; Norton, *W. A. Norton's Directory*, 325.

18. Nordin, *Rich Harvest*, 4, 6; Trump, *Grange in Michigan*, 7, 31.

19. Nordin, *Rich Harvest*, 7, 9, 31. For a helpful study from an anthropological perspective on how ritual creates community bonds, see Paul Connerton, *How Societies Remember* (Cambridge: Cambridge University Press, 1989).

20. Nordin, *Rich Harvest*, 239.

21. *Why Join the Grange?* Leaflet #2 (Springfield, MA: Grange Publicity Bureau, 1924), 1.

22. Nordin, *Rich Harvest*, 238.

23. Ibid., 239.

24. Ibid., 8.

25. Ibid., 32.

26. National Archives, pension of Nancy Seaton.

27. Georgia Underwood, unpublished written reminiscences, October 12, 1967, Covert Museum, Covert, MI.

28. *South Haven Sentinel* (South Haven, MI), April 30, 1870 (Vol. 3, no. 43), 3. (From clipping file at the Covert Museum, Covert, MI.)

29. *History of Berrien*, 438–39.

30. *Portrait and Biographical Record*, 530–35.

31. Sarno, *Covert's Heritage*, 15.

32. *Portrait and Biographical Record*, 744–45.

33. *Chatham Sesquicentennial*, n.p.

34. Dykstra, *Bright Radical Star*, 29.

35. Ibid., 28–29.

36. Ibid., 28–32; Genser, "Rigid Government," 351.

37. *Chatham Sesquicentennial*, n.p.

38. Sexton, *Congregationalism*, 8.

39. R.G. Dun and Co. Collection; U.S. Manuscript census schedules, 1880.

40. An 1850 federal census of Whitley County, IN, shows Dawson's brother Fielding having a five-year-old son called Allen in 1850. Allen Pompey shows up in the 1870 Covert census as a twenty-four-year-old mulatto man from Indiana.

41. The Covert Township federal census records from 1880 designate Allen Pompey as mulatto and his wife as white. There are no census records for 1890, but in 1900 a new census taker described Huster as mulatto. What is clear is that the original census taker in 1880 had either been informed or had perceived that Huster was white, which was enough to endanger a man of African descent in many communities across the Midwest.

42. Covert Township Mortgage Records, 1872, Covert Museum, Covert, MI.

43. *South Haven Sentinel* (South Haven, MI), August 31, 1873. (From clipping file at the Covert Museum, Covert, MI.)

44. Cox, *This Well Wooded Land*, 118, 154, 158.

45. Ibid., 158; *South Haven Sentinel* (South Haven, MI), August 30, 1873; Sarno, *Covert's Heritage*, 14.

46. *South Haven Sentinel* (South Haven, MI), August 30, 1873; Reminiscences of Georgia Underwood, October 12, 1967, Covert Museum, Covert, MI; Sarno, *Covert's Heritage*, 9.

47. R. G. Dun and Co. Collection, vol. 75, 289.

48. Jelks, "Race, Respectability," 19, 28, 50–52. Jelks notes that Hardy was a very light-skinned "mulatto" man and argues that this may have contributed to his success. His race was enough of an issue, however, that the local chapter of his Republican Party asked him to not run again, as they thought it would hurt their chances of success in the region.

49. Covert Township Voting Records, 1854 to 1896, Covert Museum, Covert, MI; School Census Records, Covert Township, Covert Museum, Covert, MI.

50. Covert Congregational Church Records, vols. 1, 3, Covert Museum, Covert, MI.

51. *History of Berrien*, 438; Covert Township Voting Records, Covert Museum, Covert, MI.

52. "Commissioner's Bond, April 1871, for I. Packard to Take the Office of Highway Commissioner," private collection of Pearl Sarno, Covert, MI. Although William Conner had to have a bond in order to hold his office, the actual document no longer exists, so there is no way to find out who backed him.

53. Covert Township Voting Records, 1875, Covert Museum, Covert, MI.

Chapter 5 Equality: 1875–1880

1. Eva Carnes, "Eva Carnes, Daughter of Covert's First Doctor, Recalls Early Days," memoir given as a gift to the Covert Museum, Covert, MI, no date. Eva could well have been named after "Little Eva," one of the main characters in *Uncle Tom's Cabin*, a book that was still immensely popular at the time of her birth.

2. Cohen, *At Freedom's Edge*, 155.

3. Lepha Gillard Wescott, "Gillard Family History," family reminiscence collection, Covert Museum, Covert, MI.

4. Ibid.

5. U.S. Manuscript census schedules, Van Buren County, MI, 1860–1920; *Census and Statistics of Michigan.*

6. The number of African American landowners was unusual for Michigan, as was the value of the land they owned. The tables are compiled from information from the Federal Agricultural Census of 1870 and 1880, and they show the amount of land owned by each black landowning farmer in those two decades. All except John Russel and M. Jackson would stay in the township until the 1890s, and most lived on their farms in Covert until their death. All were socially and politically active and prominent in Covert. Although the actual number of farms owned and operated by African Americans in one township may seem low, these numbers must be compared to the total number of farms owned and operated by African Americans in the state of Michigan.

In 1900 W. E. B. Du Bois compiled a special supplement for the 1900 census on black farmers in the United States, and he found that there were only 391 farms wholly owned and operated by African Americans in the state of Michigan. Du Bois found that white farmers owned, on average, more land than African Americans: 86.6 acres to black farmers' 61.1, a proportion similar to that in Covert. Du Bois also found, however, that the average value of a white farm was $3,404, while the average value of an African American farm was $2,303, but in Covert the value of land owned by farmers of African descent was three times higher than that of land owned by whites (Du Bois, "The Negro Farmer," 544, 578).

7. Cayton and Onuf, *Midwest and the Nation*, 46.

8. Peter Clark, as quoted in Lawrence Grossman's "In His Veins Coursed No Bootlicking Blood: The Career of Peter H. Clark," in Foner, *Reconstruction*, 471–72.

9. "Ridout and Thompson" to William Coppinger, May 29, 1879, American Colonization Society Paper, Library of Congress, as excerpted in Foner, *Reconstruction,* 608.

10. National Archives, pension of Lorenzo Pompey.

11. Genevieve Rood Bentley, "Memoirs of an Old Lady in Hurry," January 1991, n.p.; Ada Gowens, interview by Pearl Sarno, 1976, tape recording, Covert Museum, Covert, MI.

12. Mauss, *Gift,* 65, 82.

13. U.S. Manuscript census schedules, Covert Township, MI, 1870.

14. Rowland, *Van Buren County,* 476.

15. Cayton and Onuf, *Midwest and the Nation,* 46–47.

16. U.S. Manuscript census schedules, 1880. In this census, for example, John and Laura Spelman, a white couple, had a thirty-four-year-old boarder named Gertrude Enslow and an eighteen-year-old servant called Lulu Barnes, making clear that a boarder was not considered someone who worked in the home for pay or keep as a servant did.

17. U.S. Manuscript census schedules, 1870, 1880; Lake, *Atlas of Van Buren County.*

18. Vincent, *Southern Seed, Northern Soil,* 125–26.

19. Lake, *Atlas of Van Buren County.*

20. U.S. Manuscript census schedules, Covert Township, 1880.

21. To this day the Pokagons and their stories are hard to find. I am indebted to John Low, a Pokagon and the official lawyer for his people, who gently reminded me that the Pokagons, then and now, may be choosing to be separate, to live their lives privately. I chose to respect that desire for privacy. I know that, for too long, the prying eyes of the government and academics have led to lies, misinformation, and ruin for many of the First People of this country.

22. U.S. Manuscript census schedules, Covert Township, Michigan, 1880.

23. Ibid. Wesaw's name is spelled differently in almost every text I have found. Eva calls him "Weesaw," and the census taker spelled his name "Weaw" in 1880 but "Wesaw" in 1870.

24. Joseph Toquin, Weso Neota ("Wesaw Mota"), and Aseto Neota all bought forty-acre plots in Covert (then Deerfield) Township, from the federal govern-

ment, on July 24, 1854; RG80-116 Tract Books, 1818–1962 (Microfilm roll #6475), State of Michigan Archives, Lansing, MI.

25. Carnes, "Eva Carnes"; U.S. Manuscript census schedules, Covert Township, MI, 1880.

26. If African Americans are valorized and treated sympathetically by the texts in the Covert collection, Yankees fare even better. The heroic actions of the Yankees in books are often in direct contrast to those of Native Americans, whom they were usually opposing and conquering. Robert Sears's *A Pictorial Description of the United States* (New York: Robert Sears, 1855) starts with New England, thus giving primary attention to the states from which the white settlers of Covert came. Another book in Covert's collection that deals poorly with native peoples is James Lanman's *History of Michigan* (New York: E. French, 1839). Lanman describes Native Americans as "savages" who are unable to appreciate "civilization" or to become "civilized" (308–10).

27. Carnes, "Eva Carnes."

28. This phenomenon is explained in Alcorn, "Leadership and Stability," a study of the small town of Paris, Illinois, during the nineteenth century. The group most likely to control community functions in a place like Covert included those "who had been in town much longer than those they led and they stayed longer too." As in Paris, Illinois, Covert community leaders most often had to meet the criteria of "stability, wealth, occupation, and age" (701). But in Covert both African Americans and whites who met those criteria could become elites.

29. Asad, "Agency, Subject." Asad notes that even if the community's economic elites were not aware of their agency and power in creating and preserving the radical culture in Covert, this did not mean that they did not have agency. "Agency" is seen by scholars as a completed successful action, not necessarily an action or actions that were made consciously on the part of those undertaking them.

30. Jelks, "Race, Respectability," 70.

31. William Wells Brown as quoted in the *Springfield Republican* (Springfield, IL), September 4, 1874, excerpted in Blight, *Race and Reunion*, 131.

32. Blight, *Race and Reunion*, 131–38.

33. Norton, *W. A. Norton's Anthology*, 325.

34. Clawson, *Constructing Brotherhood*, 131–32; Sprague, *Constitution*, 49.

35. Padgett, "Evangelicals Divided," 256. I spent a great deal of time trying to track down the membership list for this branch of the IOOF. My search finally ended with the current head of the local organization, which had by then moved to another community, and he was unwilling to show me the documents in his care.

My grateful thanks go to Mark Noll for his input and information on Congregationalists and their relationship with fraternal organizations in the nineteenth century. Also, it should be made clear that none of the Packards ever noted their involvement in any fraternal organizations in any of their biographies. They always noted with pride, however, their involvement in the church. (Brief biographies of the Packards appear in *History of Berrien and Van Buren Counties* and *Portrait and Biographical Record,* in the bibliography.)

36. One can still go to the tiny village of Plainfield, in the Berkshire Mountains, and see the eighteenth-century church, with its high steeple and white clapboard sides, and know that its members went west and replicated their church so precisely that even the pews and benches were arranged in the same manner.

37. Rowland, *Van Buren County,* 85–86, 474, 477; *History of Berrien,* 436.

38. Covert Township Records, 1879.

39. Du Bois, *Souls of Black Folk,* 45–46.

Chapter 6 Independence: 1880–1884

1. Eugene Hardy, "Colored Citizens Celebrate," *Grand Rapids Eagle* (Grand Rapids, MI), August 2, 1883, 2, as quoted in Jelks, "Race, Respectability," 64.

2. Katchun, *Festivals of Freedom,* 3, 54.

3. Cha-Jua, *America's First Black Town,* 104–5.

4. Katchun, *Festivals of Freedom,* 4–5, 7, 26–27, 59.

5. Franklin and Moss, *From Slavery to Freedom,* 252–53.

6. Katchun, *Festivals of Freedom,* 118.

7. Ibid., 9.

8. National Archives, pension of Lorenzo Pompey.

9. The primary record for these festivals in Covert was the local paper, the *South Haven Sentinel.* Unfortunately, soon after the South Haven Library transferred

the newspaper to microfilm and destroyed the original papers, the roll containing the entire 1870s was lost, so no record survives as to when exactly these festivals started.

10. "August 2, 1881" (announcement for the South Haven Emancipation festival), *South Haven Sentinel* (South Haven, MI), July 30, 1881.

11. "C. Walter Teitsworth Recalls 1880's 4th of July Celebration," 1966, private collection of Pearl Sarno, Covert, MI.

12. According to the federal census of 1880, South Haven Township had a total population of 2,245, with 31 black residents, which meant that blacks made up only about 1 percent of the population, as opposed to the 101 African Americans in Covert at the time, who made up 9 percent of the population. The heads of household in South Haven made their wages by taking in laundry, cooking, being barbers, gardening, and working as laborers on local farms.

13. "C. Walter Teitsworth Recalls 1880's 4th of July Celebration," 1966, private collection of Pearl Sarno, Covert, MI.

14. "W. F. Conner of Covert," *South Haven Sentinel* (South Haven, MI), July 26, 1884.

15. Information from http://academic.csuohio.edu/clevelandhistory/Issue3/articles/africanamericanarchivespartone.htm and http://ech.cwru.edu/time line.html.

For those interested in learning more about John Patterson Green, his papers are held at the Western Reserve Historical Society: http://www.wrhs.org/library/template.asp?id=283.

16. Hobsbawm, "Inventing Traditions," 12.

17. The concept of blackness in Covert was further complicated by the fact that some of the "blacks" in Covert, such as the Pompeys, were very light-skinned, sometimes with green and blue eyes, even though they were often the most active in asserting a separate identity as "Negro." For example, in July of 1895, two African American families of Covert, the Pompeys and the much darker-skinned Tylers, hosted an Emancipation Day celebration that asserted to the rapidly growing population that theirs was a unique and proud identity.

In fact in Covert the Pompeys and other light-skinned African Americans seem to have *chosen* to be perceived as "Negro" by joining the Black Masonic Lodge, marching in the Juneteenth parade, and creating Emancipation Day festivities.

18. "W. F. Conner of Covert," *South Haven Sentinel* (South Haven, MI), July 26, 1884.

19. Strathern, *Gender of the Gift*, 181.

20. Frank Rood, diary, August 1, 1884, private collection of Joseph Rood, Covert, MI; "W. F. Conner of Covert," *South Haven Sentinel* (South Haven, MI), July 26, 1884.

21. J. R. Spelman, "Amusements in Early Days," unpublished document, Covert Museum, Covert, MI.

22. *South Haven Sentinel* (South Haven, MI), June 19, 1880. Lemonade, when it appeared, is specially noted by both contemporary writers and those remembering the past events at which it was served. This is not surprising, as both lemon and sugar were imported from far away and were exotic luxury goods. In addition to being a special treat, lemonade also represents the fact that Covert was far from isolated, for its citizens could get lemons and sugar, meaning that they were tied, through at least the marketplace, to the broader world.

23. DeVries, *Race and Kinship*, 153.

24. Ibid., 10.

25. Norton, *W. A. Norton's Directory*, 324–25.

26. Thornbrough, *Negro in Indiana*, 375, 378.

27. Cohen, *At Freedom's Edge*, 221–28.

28. U.S. Manuscript census schedule, Van Buren County, 1880.

29. Mortgage Book, March 29, 1883, n.p.

30. Covert Township Voting Records, 1882, 1883, Covert Museum, Covert, MI.

31. Mortgage Book, March 29, 1883, n.p.

32. Friedman, *Law in America*, 158 (n. 24).

33. Franklin and Moss, *From Slavery to Freedom*, 262.

34. Squibb, "Roads to Plessy," 29, 41, 46.

Chapter 7 Friendship: 1885–1889

1. Gertrude Enslow, autograph book, collection of the Covert Museum, Covert, MI.

2. Squibb, "Roads to Plessy," 228.

3. Arnett, "New Black Laws," 399–400.

4. David Rood's name is among those on a plaque on the wall of the Plainfield Congregational Church in Plainfield, Massachusetts. The plaque is in honor of the Reverend Moses Hallock, the first minister of that church, but it also notes more than a dozen names of people who became missionaries from the tiny community. Among them are David Rood, who worked in what was later South Africa for three decades before retiring to Covert, where David's brothers lived.

5. Frank Rood, diary, January 17 and 20 and February 15, 1884, private collection of Joseph Rood, Covert, MI.

6. *Manual of the Congregational Church of Covert Michigan*, May 25, 1888, Covert Museum, Covert, MI, n.p.

7. Numerous oral history interviews confirm this fact. Indeed, it would have been surprising, given the integrated nature of all the other social organizations in the community, for the church—founded by abolitionists—to have been segregated.

8. Gerber, *Black Ohio*, 6.

9. Prudential Committee Record Book, April 21, 1885–June 12, 1894, Covert Museum, Covert, MI.

10. National Archives, pension of Joseph and Nancy Seaton.

11. Ibid.

12. Ibid.

13. Prudential Committee Record Book, April 21, 1885–June 12, 1894, Covert Museum, Covert, MI.

14. Ibid.

15. U.S. Manuscript census schedule, Van Buren County, MI, 1880.

16. Prudential Committee Record Book, April 21, 1885–June 12, 1894, Covert Museum, Covert, MI.

17. Ibid.

18. Frank Rood, diary, inside back cover, September 28, 1887, private collection of Joseph Rood, Covert, MI.

19. U.S. Manuscript census schedule, Van Buren County, MI, 1880.

20. Blight, *Race and Reunion*, 194–95.

21. "Petition to Organize post 351, February 24, 1886," Covert Grand Army of the Republic Papers, Michigan Archives, Lansing, MI.

22. *Special Census of Union Veterans and Their Widows*, 1890 (Van Buren County, MI, Enumeration District number 283), 1–6.

23. Mason and Pentecost, *From Bull Run to Appomattox*, 61.

24. *Eighth Annual Encampment*, n.p.

25. *National Cyclopedia*, 521.

26. Le Goff, *History and Memory*, 54.

27. In all of the records published by members of the GAR, their involvement in the Civil War is always mentioned in detail. Blacks were not the only group for whom the Civil War led to a new sense of citizenship. Jacob Gunsaul, a German, was also active in the Covert GAR. He was also owner of the Covert General Store and was not only well known, but well liked. Like the black soldiers in Covert, he saw action during the war. He also had the unique experience among veterans in Covert of surviving Libby Prison, an infamous Confederate prison in Richmond, VA, where many men starved or died from the diseases that ran rampant through the weakened population (Anderson, *They Died*, 111–14).

28. Adams and Sanders, *Alienable Rights*, 229–30.

29. Vander Velde, "Michigan Supreme Court," 107, 122; Stephenson, *Race Distinctions*, 187. Blight *(Race and Reunion)* makes the compelling argument that the nation deliberately turned its back on the issues of black civil rights and racial equality in order to heal the rifts between the white North and South. He also points out that this rejection of black claims for equality was aided by an ultimately successful media war waged by racist Southern whites.

30. Waite, "Segregation of Black Students," 364.

31. For a contemporary perspective on segregation within schools, see *Why Are All the Black Kids Sitting Together in the Cafeteria?* by Beverly Daniel Tatum (New York: Basic Books, 1997).

32. Covert Township Voting Records, 1854 to 1896, Covert Museum, Covert, MI; School Census Records, Covert Township, Covert Museum, Covert, MI.

33. School administrators did start buying new textbooks in the late 1870s and early 1880s, but students in Covert's schools would have continued to read the same books, decade after decade, through those pivotal years that saw the rise of Jim Crow throughout the rest of the nation. Thus, Covert's students were repeatedly exposed to a particular moment in American history and thought that was being erased across America after the Civil War. (*Annual Report of the School Inspectors.*)

34. Blight, *Race and Reunion*, 222–25, 259–60, 277–91.

35. Boxer, "Dueling Memories," 1–10; *Annual Report of the School Inspectors.*

36. Flora Grace Reynolds, autograph book, private collection of Helen Lundie, Holland, MI.

37. Gertrude Enslow, autograph book, collection of the Covert Museum, Covert, MI.

38. Arvena Tyler, autograph book, private collection of Ernestine Carter Taitt.

Chapter 8 Justice: 1890–1896

1. John A. Dungill, "Emancipation," *South Haven Sentinel* (South Haven, MI), August 17, 1895.

2. Cohen, *At Freedom's Edge*, 211. Oliver Cox, in his book *Caste, Class and Race* (New York: Modern Reader, 1970), first published in 1948, makes a well-accepted argument that racial violence and lynching were used as tools of repression and occurred in cycles within communities. These cycles would be touched off by white perceptions that blacks were becoming too successful and powerful, a perception that could be aggravated by economic depressions. This lends a chilling rationality to the cycle of violence that occurred in the early 1890s.

3. For a brief but powerful overview of the rise of lynching in the Midwest, see "Judge Lynch in the Old Northwest" in Squibb, "Roads to Plessy," 234–43.

4. Cha-Jua, *America's First Black Town*, 16; quote from *Indianapolis Freeman*, June 10, 1893, as quoted in Squibb, "Roads to Plessy," 244.

5. "Official Directory and Program for the Silver Encampment G.A.R., Detroit, August 3d to 8th, 1891" (Executive Committee, 1891), 10, 21.

6. Berwanger, *Frontier Against Slavery*, 32; and Berwanger, "Western Anti-Negro Sentiment," 1, 90, 109–10.

7. More information and a good guide to Encampment information can be found on the Library of Congress Web site at http://www.loc.gov/rr/main/gar/national/natlist.html.

8. William Conner may have been responsible for the creation of that very ditch, for he had been elected to the position of drain commissioner in 1877, winning with ninety-two votes against his white opponent's four. His budget was a large one, as his responsibilities were daunting. He had to collect a drain tax from all taxpayers in the township and oversee the work of local men in the creation of drains. The role of drain commissioner was an important, albeit stressful, position in that swampy township (Covert Township Board Records, Covert, MI, 1887).

9. *Nelson v. Tyler*, case file 15168, record group number, 96–171, box 91 (State of Michigan Archives, Lansing, MI).

10. Ibid.

11. *South Haven Sentinel* (South Haven, MI), July 27, 1895.

12. Sarno, *Covert's Heritage*, 41–42; "Old German Baptist Brethren," 5, 66.

13. Frank Rood, diary, October 8–15, 22, 1889, private collection of Joseph Rood, Bangor, MI.

14. "Official Records of the Covert Pomological Society, 1893 to 1896," Van Buren County Historical Society, Hartford, MI.

15. *Illustrated Atlas*, n.p.; Violet Jeffries, Verna Curtis, and Faith Fennel, interview by the author, September 21, 1996, cassette tape, in author's possession.

16. Conner was not the only ranking Grange member who was black. Benjamin Gowens, who had arrived in Covert in the late 1870s, was gatekeeper, and William's daughter Clara was lady assistant steward (Norton, *W. A. Norton's Directory*, 14).

17. *Portrait and Biographical Record*, 533.

18. Certificate of reimbursement, June 22, 1892, Covert Museum, Covert, MI.

19. "Register of Scholars, Covert Congregational Sunday School," 1890–1902, Covert Museum, Covert, MI.

20. Ibid.

21. Ibid.

22. It should be noted that this friendship was not a bond between two families of Civil War veterans, as Gertie's father had not fought in the war.

23. *Special Census of Union Veterans and Their Widows*, 1890 (Van Buren County, MI, Enumeration District number 283), 1–6. U.S. Manuscript census schedules, 1900. There is some question as to Alice's identity. She married a white man in Covert and lived there till her death. Elderly white members of the community had thought she was white, but she is almost certainly the twenty-two-year-old Alice Adams, the only "Alice" in the 1900 census whose age would match that of the young woman in the photo. Alice and both of her parents are listed in the 1900 census as "black," although it should be noted that "black" was the only racial designation given to people of African descent, regardless of the color of their skin, in that census.

24. "Cavanaugh Family of Michigan," *The Political Graveyard,* online source available at http://politicalgraveyard.com/families/3143.html (December 5, 2004).

25. *Nelson v. Tyler,* case file 15168, record group number, 96–171, box 91 (State of Michigan Archives, Lansing, MI). On January 14, 1896, the state supreme court decided to try the case. The complete proceedings are also published in *Michigan Supreme Court Records and Briefs,* January term, 1896, 105–18.

26. Ibid.

27. Helen Lundie, who was raised by her grandparents in Covert, recalled that her grandfather often told her a cautionary tale about racist language. His story dated from the period the trial took place. He was good friends with the Pompeys, and one day a member of the Pompey family came by when the grandfather was painting his house. Mr. Pompey complimented him on his job, and pleased, the grandfather replied, "It shines like a nigger's heel." As soon as he said it, "he felt awful" and apologized profusely to Mr. Pompey. He often followed this story up with one in which he recounted being injured while in Chicago at a GAR Encampment. Alone in a strange hospital in that big city, the only person who came to visit him was the young wife of one of the Pompey clan, now married to a minister in Chicago (oral history interview with Helen Lundie, 1998, transcript in author's possession).

28. *Nelson v. Tyler,* case file 15168, record group number, 96–171, box 91 (State of Michigan Archives, Lansing, MI).

29. Adams and Sanders, *Alienable Rights,* 243–45.

30. *South Haven Sentinel* (South Haven, MI), August 18, 1894, and July 27, 1895.

31. This information on John Langston was found on a number of excellent Web sites, including the African American Registry's Web site at http://www.aaregistry.com/african_american_history/482/John_M_Langston_Americas_first_elected_Black_politician and the biographical directory of the United States Congress, which also includes a bibliography of publications on Langston at http://bioguide.congress.gov/scripts/biodisplay.pl?index=L000074.

32. The involvement of the local press in the covering of these festivities of freedom is significant in that they were able to give a narrative that helped to shape how those in Covert saw their community, as well as those outside of the township. Editors and writers of local papers, through their coverage of certain events, could be actively involved in the creation of a community's identity as well as of certain groups within that community. So it is important that the local paper chose to cover Covert's Emancipation festivals, both for the creation of African Americans' self-constructed identity as well as Covert's communal identity as one that was unusual and even radical (Conzen, "Pi-ing the Type," 93).

33. John A. Dungill, "Emancipation," *South Haven Sentinel* (South Haven, MI), August 17, 1895.

34. Ibid.

35. Ibid.

36. Ibid.

37. *Nelson v. Tyler*, case file 15168, record group number, 96–171, box 91 (State of Michigan Archives, Lansing, MI).

38. *National Cyclopedia of American Biography*, 521.

39. *Nelson v. Tyler*, case file 15168, record group number, 96–171, box 91 (State of Michigan Archives, Lansing, MI).

40. Ibid.

41. John A. Dungill, "Emancipation," *South Haven Sentinel* (South Haven, MI), August 17, 1895.

Notes

Epilogue

1. Payne, *I've Got the Light,* 5.

2. Sarno, *Covert's Heritage,* 66–67.

3. *South Haven Sentinel* (South Haven, MI), September 24, 1898.

4. Ibid.

5. U.S. Manuscript census schedules, Van Buren County, MI, 1900; Norton, *W. A. Norton's Directory,* 134–55; *Standard Atlas,* n.p.

6. *Morning Sentinel* (South Haven, MI), August 15, 1901.

7. *South Haven Messenger* (South Haven, MI), February 18, 1898, and April 1, 1898.

8. U.S. Manuscript census schedules, Van Buren County, MI, 1910.

9. Squibb, "Roads to Plessy," 76; Voegeli, *Free But Not Equal,* 2, 172.

10. Squibb, "Roads to Plessy," 79.

11. Gerber, *Black Ohio,* 207

12. Franklin and Moss, *From Slavery to Freedom,* 315–17.

13. Ibid., 315–17; Thornbrough, *The Negro in Indiana,* 284–86; Robinson, "Oklahoma," 2045, 2047. Also see Scott Ellsworth, *Death in a Promised Land: The Tulsa Race Riot of 1921* (Baton Rouge: Louisiana State University Press, 1992).

14. For an excellent overview of how the Midwest led the way in constructing legal precedent for segregation, see Squibb, "Roads to Plessy."

15. My thanks to Sara Austin for pointing out the question "Why not?"

16. Vincent, *Southern Seed, Northern Soil,* xii.

17. Violet Jeffries, interview by the author, November 9, 1996, cassette tape, in author's possession.

18. Cohen (*Making of the New Deal*) makes a similar and potent argument (8, 367).

Bibliography

Adams, Francis, and Barry Sanders. *Alienable Rights*. New York: HarperCollins, 2003.

Alcorn, Richard. "Leadership and Stability in Mid-Nineteenth-Century America: A Case Study of an American Town." *Journal of American History* 61 (December 1974): 685–702.

Anderson, William. *They Died to Make Men Free: A History of the Nineteenth Michigan Infantry in the Civil War*. Berrien Springs, MI: Hardscrabble, 1980.

Annual Report of the School Inspectors of the Township of Deerfield, County of Van Buren, for the year 1864. State of Michigan Archives, Lansing.

Arnett, Benjamin. "The New Black Laws." In *The African American Archive*, edited by Kai Wright. New York: Black Dog and Leventhal, 2001.

Asad, Talal. "Agency, Subject, and the Body." Paper presented at the conference "The Body: A Retrospective" at the University of Manchester, Manchester, England, June 1998.

Ballou, John. *The Lady of the West; or, The Gold Seekers*. Cincinnati: Moore, Wilstach, Keys, and Overend, 1855.

Bates, Samual. *History of Pennsylvania Volunteers, 1861–65*. Vol. 5. Harrisburg, PA: B. Singerly State Printers, 1869.

Benson, Susan. "Asians Have Culture, West Indians Have Problems: Discourses of Race and Ethnicity In and Out of Anthropology." Unpublished essay, Haddon Library, University of Cambridge, UK, 1994.

Berlin, Ira. *Many Thousands Gone: The First Two Centuries of Slavery in North America*. Cambridge, MA: Belknap, 1998.

———. *Slaves without Masters*. New York: Pantheon, 1974.

Berwanger, Eugene. *The Frontier Against Slavery: Western Anti-Negro Prejudice and the Slavery Extension Controversy.* Urbana: University of Illinois Press, 1967.

————. "Western Anti-Negro Sentiment and Laws, 1846–1860, A Factor in the Slavery Extension Controversy." PhD diss., Illinois State University, 1965.

Blight, David. *Race and Reunion: The Civil War in American Memory.* Cambridge, MA: Belknap, 2001.

Bogue, Allan. "An Agricultural Empire." In *The Oxford History of the American West,* edited by Clyde Milner II, Carol O'Connor, and Martha Sandweiss, 275–314. New York: Oxford University Press, 1994.

Boxer, Daniel. "Dueling Memories: The Retelling of the Civil War in the Textbooks of Boston and Richmond, 1865–1915." Senior thesis, Amherst College, 2000.

Brown, Richard Maxwell. "Violence." In *The Oxford History of the American West,* edited by Clyde Milner II, Carol O'Connor, and Martha Sandweiss, 393–426. New York: Oxford University Press, 1994.

Carpenter, Charles. *History of American Schoolbooks.* Philadelphia: University of Pennsylvania Press, 1963.

Cayton, Andrew, and Susan Gray, eds. *The American Midwest.* Bloomington: Indiana University Press, 2001.

Cayton, Andrew, and Peter Onuf. *The Midwest and the Nation: Rethinking the History of an American Region.* Bloomington: Indiana University Press, 1990.

Census and Statistics of the State of Michigan, 1884. Vol. 1. Lansing, MI: Thorp and Godfrey, 1886.

Census and Statistics of the State of Michigan, 1894. Vol. 1. Lansing, MI: Robert Smith, 1896.

Cha-Jua, Sundiata Keita. *America's First Black Town: Brooklyn, Illinois, 1830–1915.* Urbana: University of Illinois Press, 2000.

Chatham Sesquicentennial: 1881–1968. Chatham, OH: Chatham Congregational Church, 1968.

Clawson, Mary Ann. *Constructing Brotherhood: Class, Gender, and Fraternalism.* Princeton, NJ: Princeton University Press, 1989.

Clifton, James. *The Pokagons, 1683–1983: Catholic Potawatomi Indians of the St. Joseph River Valley.* Lanham, MD: University Press of America, 1984.

Coe, David, ed. *Mine Eyes Have Seen the Glory: Combat Diaries of Union Sergeant Hamlin Alexander Coe.* Madison, WI: Fairleigh Dickinson University Press, 1975.

Cohen, Lizabeth. *Making of the New Deal: Industrial Workers in Chicago, 1919–1939.* Cambridge: Cambridge University Press, 1991.

Cohen, William. *At Freedom's Edge.* Baton Rouge: Louisiana State University Press, 1991.

Conzen, Katherine. "Pi-ing the Type: Jane Grey Swisshelm and the Contest of Midwest Regionality." In Cayton and Gray, *The American Midwest: Essays on Regional History,* 91–110. Bloomington: Indiana University Press, 2001.

Cox, Anna-Lisa. "Nineteenth-Century African Americans." In *The Encyclopedia of the Midwest.* Bloomington: Indiana University Press, 2005.

Cox, Thomas. *This Well Wooded Land: Americans and their Forests from Colonial Times to the Present.* Lincoln: University of Nebraska Press, 1985.

DeVries, James. *Race and Kinship in a Midwestern Town: The Black Experience in Monroe, Michigan, 1900–1915.* Urbana: University of Illinois Press, 1984.

Du Bois, W. E. Burghardt. "The Negro Farmer." In *Department of Commerce and Labor Bureau of the Census Special Reports Supplementary Analysis and Derivative Tables, Twelfth Census of the United States, 1900.* Washington, DC: Government Printing Office, 1906.

Du Bois, W. E. Burghardt. *The Souls of Black Folk.* New York: Signet Classic, 1995.

Dyer, Frederick. *Compendium of the War of the Rebellion.* Des Moines, IA: Dyer, 1908.

Dykstra, Robert. *Bright Radical Star: Black Freedom and White Supremacy on the Hawkeye Frontier.* Cambridge, MA: Harvard University Press, 1993.

Eighth Annual Encampment of the Department of Michigan Grand Army of the Republic. Flint, MI: Eddy, 1886.

Foner, Eric. *Reconstruction: America's Unfinished Revolution, 1865–1877.* New York: Harper and Row, 1988.

———. "Slavery, the Civil War, and Reconstruction." In *The New American History,* edited by Eric Foner, 85–106. Philadelphia: Temple University Press, 1997.

Formisano, Ronald. "The Edge of Caste: Colored Suffrage in Michigan, 1827–1861." *Michigan History* 46 (Spring 1972): 19–41.

Franklin, John Hope, and Alfred Moss Jr. *From Slavery to Freedom: A History of African Americans.* New York: Knopf, 1994.

Friedman, Lawrence. *Law in America.* New York: Modern Library, 2002.

Genser, Wallace. "'A Rigid Government Over Ourselves': Transformations in Ethnic, Gender, and Race Consciousness on the Northern Borderlands — Michigan, 1805–1865." PhD diss., University of Michigan, 1998.

Gerber, David. *Black Ohio and the Color Line: 1860–1915.* Urbana: University of Illinois Press, 1976.

Gjerde, Jon. *The Minds of the West.* Chapel Hill: University of North Carolina Press, 1997.

Gray, Susan. *The Yankee West: Community Life on the Michigan Frontier.* Chapel Hill: University of North Carolina Press, 1996.

Hart, James. *The Oxford Companion to American Literature.* Oxford: Oxford University Press, 1995.

Heinegg, Paul. "Free African Americans of Virginia, North Carolina, South Carolina, Maryland and Delaware." http://www.freeafricanamericans.com.

Hesslink, George K. *Black Neighbors: Negroes in a Northern Rural Community.* New York: Bobbs-Merrill, 1968.

Hildreth, Richard. *The White Slave.* Boston: J. H. Eastburn, 1836.

Hinderaker, Eric. "Liberating Contrivances: Narrative and Identity in Midwestern History." In Cayton and Gray, *The American Midwest: Essays on Regional Culture,* 48–68. Bloomington: Indiana University Press, 2001.

History of Berrien and Van Buren Counties, Michigan. Philadelphia: D. W. Ensign, 1880.

Hobsbawm, Eric. "Inventing Traditions." In *The Invention of Tradition,* edited by Eric Hobsbawm and Terence Ranger, 1–14. Cambridge: Cambridge University Press, 1983.

Holt, Thomas. "African-American History." In *The New American History,* edited by Eric Foner, 311–31. Philadelphia: Temple University Press, 1997.

Horton James, and Lois Horton. *In Hope of Liberty: Culture, Community, and Protest among Northern Free Blacks.* New York: Oxford University Press, 1997.

Illustrated Atlas of Van Buren County, Michigan. Racine, WI: Kace, 1895.

Jelks, Randal. "Race, Respectability, and the Struggle for Civil Rights: A Study of the African American Community of Grand Rapids, Michigan, 1870–1954." PhD diss., Michigan State University, 1999.

Katchun, Mitch. *Festivals of Freedom*. Amherst: University of Massachusetts Press, 2003.

Kirkland, Caroline. *A New Home, Who'll Follow?* Edited by Sandra Zaggarell. New Brunswick, NJ: Rutgers University Press, 1990.

Lake, D. J. *Atlas of Van Buren County, Michigan*. Philadelphia: C. O. Titus, 1873.

Lanman, James. *History of Michigan*. New York: E. French, 1839.

Larson, John Lautritz. "Pigs in Space; or, What Shapes America's Regional Cultures?" In Cayton and Gray, *The American Midwest: Essays on Regional Culture*, 69–77. Bloomington: Indiana University Press, 2001.

Le Goff, Jacques. *History and Memory*. Translated by Steven Rendall. New York: Columbia University Press, 1992.

Lind, Michael. *What Lincoln Believed*. New York: Doubleday, 2004.

Litwack, Leon. *North of Slavery: The Negro in the Free States, 1790–1860*. Chicago: University of Chicago Press, 1961.

Long, Clarence. *Wages and Earnings in the United States, 1860–1890*. Princeton, NJ: Princeton University Press, 1960.

Martin, Edgar W. *The Standard of Living in 1860: American Consumption on the Eve of the Civil War*. Chicago: University of Chicago Press, 1942.

Mason, Phillip, and Paul Pentecost. *From Bull Run to Appomattox: Michigan's Role in the Civil War*. Detroit: Wayne State University Press, 1961.

Mauss, Marcel. *The Gift: The Form and Reason for Exchange in Archaic Societies*. London: Routledge, 1990.

McCaul, Robert. *The Black Struggle for Public Schooling in Nineteenth-Century Illinois*. Carbondale: Southern Illinois University, 1987.

National Archives, Washington, DC. Civil War Pension Files, Records of the Veterans Administration. RG15. Civil War Pension of Himebrick Tyler, C.W. 393634; Civil War Pension of Nancy Seaton, C.W. 339165; Civil War Pension of William F. Conner, C.W. 561549; Civil War Pension of Lorenzo Pompey, C.W. 901921; Washington L. Pompey Pension Claim, C.W. 625630.

National Cyclopedia of American Biography. New York: J. T. White, 1937.

Nordin, D. Sven. *Rich Harvest: A History of the Grange, 1867–1900*. Jackson: University of Mississippi Press, 1974.

Norton, Willard A. *W. A. Norton's Directory of South Haven, Casco, and Covert, 1898 to 1900*. South Haven, MI: W. A. Norton, 1898.

Padgett, Chris. "Evangelicals Divided: Abolition and the Plan of Union's Demise in Ohio's Western Reserve." In *Religion and the Antebellum Debate over Slavery*, edited by John McKivigan and Michael Snay, 249–72. Athens: University of Georgia Press, 1998.

Painter, Nell Irvin. *Sojourner Truth, A Life, A Symbol*. New York: W. W. Norton, 1996.

Payne, Charles M. *I've Got the Light of Freedom*. Berkeley: University of California Press, 1995.

———. "'The Whole United States is Southern!': *Brown v. Board* and the Mystification of Race." *Journal of American History* 91 (June 2004): 83–91.

Portrait and Biographical Record of Kalamazoo, Allegan, and Van Buren Counties, Michigan. Chicago: Chapman Brothers, 1892.

Reynolds, David. *John Brown: Abolitionist*. New York: Knopf, 2005.

R. G. Dun and Co. Collection. Baker Library, Harvard University Graduate School of Business Administration, Boston.

Robertson, Jno. *Michigan in the War*. Lansing, MI: W. S. George, State Binders and Printers, 1882.

Robinson, Greg. "Oklahoma." In the *Encyclopedia of African American Culture and History*. Vol. 4. Edited by Jack Salzman, David Smith, and Cornel West, 2043–48. New York: Macmillan Library Reference, 1996.

Robinson, Marilynne. *The Death of Adam*. New York: Houghton Mifflin, 1998.

Rowland, O. W. *A History of Van Buren County, Michigan*. Chicago: Lewis, 1912.

Rubenstein, Bruce, and Lawrence Ziewacz. *Michigan: A History of the Great Lakes State*. St. Louis, MO: Forum, 1981.

Sarno, Pearl. *A Look at Covert's Heritage*. South Haven, MI: Sarno, 1976.

Satz, Ronald. "Indian Policy in the Jacksonian Era: The Old Northwest as a Test Case." *Michigan History* 60 (1976): 71–93.

Sawyer, Marcia. "Surviving Freedom: African American Farm Households in Cass County, Michigan, 1832–1880." PhD diss., Michigan State University, 1990.

Sexton, Jessie Ethelyn. *Congregationalism, Slavery, and the Civil War*. Lansing: Michigan Civil War Centennial Observance Commission, 1966.

Special Census of Union Veterans and their Widows, 1890. Van Buren County, MI, Enumeration District Number 283. Washington, DC: Government Printing Office.

Sprague, Jonathan. *Constitution, By-Laws of the Grand Lodge I.O.O.F., of the State of Michigan.* Ann Arbor, MI: Curier Book and Job Printing House, 1884.

Squibb, John. "Roads to Plessy: Blacks and the Law in the Old Northwest: 1860–1896." PhD diss., University of Wisconsin, 1992.

Standard Atlas of Van Buren County, Michigan. Chicago: Geo. A. Ogle, 1912.

Statistics of the State of Michigan. Lansing, MI: W. S. George, State Printers and Binders, 1873.

Stephenson, Gilbert. *Race Distinctions in American Law.* New York: Negro Universities Press, 1969.

Stewart, Roma Jones. "The Migration of a Free People." *Michigan History* 71 (1987): 34–39.

Stowe, Harriet Beecher. *Dred: A Tale of the Great Dismal Swamp.* Edited by Judy Newman. Edinburgh: University of Edinburgh Press, 1999.

Strathern, Marilyn. *The Gender of the Gift: Problems with Women and Problems with Society in Melanesia.* Berkeley: University of California Press, 1988.

Tanner, Helen Hornbook, ed. *Atlas of Great Lakes Indian History.* Norman: University of Oklahoma Press, 1987.

Thornbrough, Emma Lou. *The Negro in Indiana: A Study of a Minority.* Indianapolis: Indiana Historical Bureau, 1957.

Tiffany, Alexander. *A Treatise on the Powers and Duties of Justices of the Peace in the State of Michigan.* Adrian, MI: Power Press of R. W. Ingals, 1850.

Trudeau, Noah. *Like Men of War: Black Troops in the Civil War, 1862–1865.* Boston: Little, Brown, 1998.

Trump, Fred. *The Grange in Michigan.* Grand Rapids, MI: 1963.

Turner, Victor. "Introduction." In *Celebration: Studies in Festival and Ritual,* edited by Victor Turner, 11–32. Washington, DC: Smithsonian Institution Press, 1982.

———. *Dramas, Fields, and Metaphors: Symbolic Action in Human Society.* Ithaca, NY: Cornell University Press, 1974.

Vander Velde, Lewis. "The Michigan Supreme Court Defines Negro Rights, 1866–1869." In *Michigan Perspectives: People, Events, and Issues,* edited by Alan Brown, John Houdek, and John Yzenbaard, 105–26. Dubuque, IA: Kendall/Hunt, 1974.

Vincent, Stephen. *Southern Seed, Northern Soil: African American Farm Communities in the Midwest, 1765–1900.* Bloomington: University of Indiana Press, 1999.

Voegeli, V. Jacque. *Free But Not Equal: The Midwest and the Negro During the Civil War.* Chicago: University of Chicago Press, 1967.

Waite, Cally. "The Segregation of Black Students at Oberlin College after Reconstruction." *History of Education Quarterly* 41, no. 3 (2001): 344–64.

Walker, Juliet. *Free Frank: A Black Pioneer in the Antebellum Frontier.* Lexington: University Press of Kentucky, 1983.

White, Richard. *The Middle Ground.* Cambridge: Cambridge University Press, 1991.

Williams, Loretta J. *Black Freemasonry and Middle-Class Realities.* Columbia: University of Missouri Press, 1980.

Wilson, Benjamin. *A Rural Black Heritage between Chicago and Detroit: 1850–1929.* Kalamazoo: New Issue Press, Western Michigan University, 1985.

Wright, Richard. *12 Million Black Voices.* New York: Thunder's Mouth Press, 2002.

Zinn, Howard. *A People's History of the United States, 1492 to the Present.* New York: HarperCollins, 1999.

Index

Independent Order of Odd Fellows (IOOF), 131–34, 145, 245n. 35

Indiana: and abolitionists, 15, 16; and Black Codes, 68, 71, 175; black population of, 68, 69, 175; and civil rights, 66; and Grand Army of the Republic, 174–75; and miscegenation laws, 205; Potawatomi people of, 40; and slavery, 10; and Underground Railroad, 20; whites in, 41

indigenous people: civil rights of, 90; in Covert, 116, 117, 127–29; of Great Lakes region, 30, 31, 231n. 61; in literature, 128, 244n. 26; Pokagons, 40, 41–42, 90, 127–28, 243n. 21; removal of, 31–32, 40

interracial marriages, 3, 108, 204–6, 241n. 41

Iowa, 15, 16, 22–25, 39, 48, 67–68

Irish immigrants, 26, 79

Jackson, M., 222, 242n. 6

Jackson family, 120

Jamison, Gertrude, 91–92

Jamison, Maggie, 91–92

Jamison, Samual, 91–92

Jefferson, Thomas, 12–13

Jeffries, John, 157, 161

Jeffries, Violet, 211

Jim Crow, 4, 83, 153–54, 165–66, 200, 207. *See also* segregation

Jones, J. W., 145

Jones, Peter, 202

Jones, William, 76–77, 145

Juneteenth festivals, 137

Kalamazoo, Michigan, 139–40

Kansas: and Brown, 17, 28; and free/ slave option, 10, 27–28, 67; violence in, 28, 67, 81, 99, 172

Kansas-Nebraska Act, 26–27

Keemer, William, 126–27

Kelley, Oliver Hudson, 100

Kenney, Ada, 171

Kentucky, 68

King, Martin Luther, Jr., 140

Kirkland, Caroline, 35

Know-Nothing Party, 26

Ku Klux Klan, 101, 175, 208, 233n. 23

Lady of the West or The Gold Seekers, The (Ballou), 78–80

Lake Michigan, 40, 109, 110, 119, 138, 148

landownership in Covert: black landownership, 50, 56, 63, 64, 71, 73, 76, 84, 85, 91, 92, 114, 120–21, 220, 221, 222, 242n. 6; white landownership, 120–21, 220, 242n. 6

Langston, John M., 193–94

Lawrence, Kansas, 28, 98–99

Liggon, Richard, 22

Lincoln, Abraham, 27, 137, 139

Long, Charles, 164–65, 197–98

Louisiana, 11, 20, 97–98

Lovejoy, Elijah, 28

Low, John, 243n. 21

Lundie, Helen, 252n. 27

Lundy, Benjamin, 14

lynchings, 88, 126–27, 173–74, 206, 250n. 2

Lyon, Horatio, 157

Maine, 26–27

Marshal, Mary, 82

Maryland, 36

Massachusetts, 27, 105

Massachusetts Fifty-fourth Colored Regiment, 58

Massachusetts Fifty-fifth Colored Regiment, 58, 59

Matthews, Louisa, 61

Mauss, Marcel, 122–23

Maxham, Harry, 204–5

Maxham, Jessie, 204–5

May, Charles, 140

Index

272

About the Author

ANNA-LISA COX is the recipient of numerous awards for her research, including the National Endowment for the Humanities Younger Scholars Award, the Gilder Lehrman Foundation Fellowship, and the Pew Younger Scholars Fellowship. She received her MPhil in social anthropology from the University of Cambridge and her PhD in American history from the University of Illinois. She is an active historian, writer, and lecturer on the history of race relations in the nineteenth-century Midwest. She is currently a scholar in residence at the Newberry Library.